THE BOOK OF GHOULBRAHAM

The Book of
GHOULBRAHAM

A GOD FROM THE PAST, PRESENT, AND THE FUTURE

GHOULBRAHAM HIMSELF

Seemingly Pointless

Contents

Prologue

Sometimes people do things to their fellow beings without thinking of what their actions would do in the lives of others. They do not get to feel the pains of others until they are being treated in like manners. They believe everything about the world revolves around the world and ends in the world. They also believe that the troubled have no one that would come to their aids so they maltreat them like they are animals. And when the immortals start fighting for them, they beg for mercy. But, when this mercy is not granted, they see the immortals as being cruel.

Sometimes most of the things that happened to us are things that have been sanctioned to happen even before we were born. It is important for us to know that it is not a must we understand everything that happens to us. We are to understand the ones our creator has given us the ability to understand, and let go of the ones they chose to hide from us.

Life is sweet and love is sweeter, live well and do not inflict pains on anyone because the day their god would come for vengeance, you will not be forgiven.

***

"Why don't you want me into your house?" Ghoulbraham, a green three-eyed creature asked a young man who was at the entrance of a gate.

"I cannot let you in because you all full of evil." The man at the gate replied Ghoulbraham as he put a lock on the gate.

"If you do not allow me come in, I will hunt you all the days of your life... not just you, but also the entire community as the souls of the ones they unjustly killed, cry up daily for vengeance." Ghoulbraham replied in anger as he pulled the gate, and the young man woke up from his sleep.

"Another nightmare!"

1

Once upon a time in the land of **INOKO, a land where every of its inhabitants have two eyes, hair on their heads, and are either blue or purple in color, a time before our time and a time before the times of time before,** lived a young creature, an orphan who was loved by majority of the villagers. Zizo lost his parents the same night when some bigger creatures from a distant town invaded their village in a reprisal attack that left many dead from both sides. He was lucky to have escaped death that night because his mother, who was the chief priestess of the village, hid him at the back of their house behind a tall tree... a tree that even when Zizo was fully grown up, never stop sitting under it for relaxation. Sitting under the tree gave Zizo immeasurable joy, as he would often fantasize him playing with his parents. The inhabitants of INOKO loved Zizo not because his late parents were kindhearted, not because Zizo was one of the most handsome young being in the village, but because he was kind to all and maintained a good relationship with them.

His name was **ZIZO.** Zizo never heard back whatever was requested of him from them. Although young and with a good skin, he was not lazy. He worked effortlessly in his farm so he would not go begging for food from the village inhabitants. There was absolutely nothing Zizo could not do. Due to his hard-working spirit, love and kind nature, every maiden, (including the married ones) desired to have him as a husband. Different passes were made at him but he never gave in to them and that made the ladies that were doing this wondered if he was normal or had something he was hiding from the villages. Some of the men weren't left out as they were not only jealous of him, but started growing hatred within their hearts for him due to the fact that their wives always called his name in their various homes, and compared them with Zizo in a way of trying to encourage them to be hard working.

One day, just as the day was waking up and the birds were getting ready for their usual morning songs, Zizo got up from his sleep. He went to the backyard of his house where he had his kitchen and a bowl of stream water from which he usually cleaned his face while making his morning prayers. He took the bowl of stream water in his left hand and using his right; he washed his face and then made his morning prayers. Although he never attended any gathering that had to do with the gods of the land, he was a strong believer of their existence and this made the gods of the land to love him as well. After his prayers, he walked back to the facade of his house and standing on his toes, he reached out to his farming implements that were in the ceiling of his house.

"Let me hurry to the farm and do some harvesting before the sun will come out." He said wearing a smile on his face.

The sun that shone in the village of Inoko was not like the sun in other villages. It usually came out very early and shone brighter in this village than in any other village and this also contributed to the lazy attitudes of the village men towards farm works. They believed the sun wasn't fair to them as it always came out early, not giving them a desirable time to sleep, scotched their backs while bending to work on their farms, and going back into the clouds after the day would have exhausted. However, some of the village men got used to it; one of such men was **TUNA**. Tuna was Zizo's friend who oftentimes was seen with Zizo either chatting, cracking jokes, making gest of themselves, eating and sometimes sleeping in each other's place. Tuna was the only son of one of the well-respected men of the village due to his exposure. He was the only one that had gone out of the village. He was rich and famous in the village. He had many farmlands with many vassals that are working under him. Tuna never allowed his father's wealth get into his head as he would always follow Zizo to the farm, and they would work on each other's farmland. His father's farm was close to Zizo's. It was a normal routine for them to go fishing after working in the farmland, not because they wanted to catch fishes but because they wanted to cool off their skin in the stream, as its water is usually cool in the afternoon. They would tell stories of how they wanted their future to be.

Just as Zizo journeyed to his farmland with his farming implements hoe, that was resting on his right shoulder, and a basket that had fishing lines and hooks in it, on his head. He heard his name from a distance.

"Who is it that is screaming my name at this time of the day?" He turned around and saw Tuna running towards him from a distance.

He blamed himself for not waiting for him at his house so both of them would go fishing. Quickly he started thinking of what to tell Tuna for not waiting for him.

"Hi, Zizo." Tuna said as he caught up with.

"Hi." Zizo replied scratching his head with the finger nails on his right hand.

He quickly apologized for not waiting for Tuna at his house so both of them would go farming and fishing together. Tuna gave him a smile saying he was not angry with him, as it must have escaped his mind. He asked Zizo where he was going to with the farm implements he was carrying. Zizo looked at him with surprise and then answered he was going to his farm to harvest some of his matured crops before the scotching sun would rise to its peak. Tuna was shocked at his answer, but, then reminded him of what the day was, a day set aside for the annual cleansing of the village and that the king has summoned everyone in the village to be at his palace as it is with the tradition of the village. Zizo told him he was not going to attend as he was had no food at home to feed on. Tuna begged he followed him so they both would attend the gathering of all the villagers at the king's palace and that he would give Zizo enough food that would last him for the day. But Zizo declined his kind gesture, placing his right hand on Tuna's shoulder; he told him that going to farm makes him healthier and stronger by the day. He also told him that if he did not go to his farm, some farm animals would eat up his matured crops. Tuna agreed with him and then decided to follow him to the farm, as it was their tradition.

Zizo rebuked Tuna from following him to the farm saying that his father would be mad at him if he did not see him at the palace and that he did not want to be the cause of a disagreement between Tuna and his father who never for once liked their friendship. Tuna gave Zizo a long smile and then assured him that his father would do no sure thing to him, as he was his only child and his heir to everything he owned. He assured Zizo that so long, he still had air in his nostrils, he would forever cherish the friendship he had with Zizo as no one in the village seems to understand him better than the way Zizo did. Upon hearing these words, Zizo dropped his farming implements and then gave Tuna a tight hug.

"Thanks for being such a great friend Tuna, may our friendship last forever, amen." Zizo said still hugging Tuna.

"Now let go of me, we have some crops to harvest in your farm today." Tuna said, disengaging himself from Zizo's grip.

Zizo released his grip on him, picked up his farming implements from the ground and they journeyed to Zizo's farm chatting on how they would want their future to be like.

2

Still in the morning and the sun was beginning to come out of his hiding place revealing the tall shadows of the trees that were in the king's compound, which gave the palace nature's beautification. The birds were singing joyfully as villagers in their twos and threes troop into the king's compound, all wearing smiling faces. Tuna's dad wearing his most expensive apparel gorgeously walked into the king's compound with some of his servants walking behind him. He soon got for himself his usual sitting position. He barely had taken a sit when the great king of Inoko came out of his chamber with the village chief priest following from behind as if someone had briefed them of his arrival. Every hand present in the compound were raised up in excitement as the king came out. The inhabitants of Inoko saw their king as their savior because he was the only warrior that came back alive from the great battle of freedom that led to the death of Zizo's parents.

They regarded him as Inoko itself even though he was not a blue blood, and his name was not Inoko but **KATINU**. They carry out every of his commands without questioning if it was to benefit the entire village or not, not because he was a good king to them, but because they believed that he was the reason why the village was still standing. In fact, they counted it a blessing from the gods to behold his face as he was always in his palace where he gave out orders.

"Greetings to you my lovely people of Inoko." Said Katinu lifting up his hands to calm the people.

He thanked them for honoring his call and keeping to the tradition of the village. Tuna's dad did not pay attention to what King Katinu was saying, as he was busy combing the large crowd with his eyes to see if his son, Tuna was present. When he was satisfied with his search, he turned to the servant at his right hand and inquired the where about of Tuna. The servant told him he did not know but that he had seen Tuna hurriedly walking out of the compound in the morning and that he was very sure he had gone farming with Zizo. Tuna's dad was angered; he tried attempting to stand up and leave the king's palace but was quickly reminded by the servant that it was a taboo to walk out on the king, especially when there was an important matter on ground.

He sat back on his chair, staring at the king but not hearing what he was saying as his mind was already on what he would do to Tuna when he returns. King Katinu apologized to them for not always having the opportunity to seeing his face whenever they wanted to and then promised to do something about it.

He reminded them the reason why they were at his palace and hope they all complied with whatever the chief priest of the village would tell them. Barely had he finished his lines when the people chorused, "WE WILL."

King Katinu sat on his royal seat that was made with leaves, not just any leaves, but the most beautiful leaves in the village to suit his royal status.

The chief priest cleared his throat and then saluted the people. He reminded them how the gods of the land have been faithful to them by not only making their lands fertile, but also making them experience peace in the village, and not experiencing attacks from neighboring villages. Everyone that was present, including the king, gave a nod in agreement, to what the chief priest said.

"They have done their parts; let's do ours by doing what they have asked us to do. They have not asked us to sacrifice any of our loved ones as in the days of our ancestors, or give them what we cherish most like they did in previous years. All they have asked us to do is to stay away from our farmlands for seven days. I mean, no one is allowed to harvest any crop in the next seven days as the gods would be feasting on the crops in our farms as a well of nourishing it for better productivity."

He told them not to hesitate in coming to the palace for foods if they should run short of food in their homes during this period. The people, especially some faction of the men gave a loud roar of happiness, knowing that they would not have to experience the scotching sun, but visit the palace to get free foods for themselves and families.

"Do you know sometimes I don't feel like bathing at home but in this stream?" Tuna asked Zizo as they both bath in the stream.

Zizo gave him a smile and then tried catching a fish that was swimming towards him.

"Sometimes, I just wish I could stay all day in this stream." Zizo said after his failed attempt to catch the fish.

Just as he was to make another attempt on a bigger fish, he heard someone singing from the other side of the stream. He paused to get a better hearing of the voice.

"Are you okay?" Tuna asked Zizo.

Zizo asked him if he was not hearing a voice that was coming from the other side of the stream. He shook his head and then answered him no. Tuna asked him to forget out the strange voice that he was not hearing, but tell him about the dream he wanted to tell him on their way to the stream. For a second, Zizo did not hear him as he was still trying to trace the direction of the voice. Tuna brought him back to his senses by slashing water on him.

"Did you say something?" Zizo asked trying to wipe clean his face with his right hand.

"I want you to tell me the dream you wanted to tell me while we were coming to the stream." Tuna said to Zizo.

"Oh, that!" Zizo exclaimed placing his both hands on his waist.

"I don't know why I keep seeing a baby, a replica of me but with green body and three eyes in my dream. Each time I see him, he would stretch out his hands like beckoning on me to come and play with him, and if I refuse playing with him, he would mess up the entire place and then give me a look that sends ice running in my spine." Zizo said wearing a confused look on his face.

Tuna too was not left out of the confusion as he had never in his entire life heard of such a dream. He asked Zizo to visit the chief priest of the village as he was in the best position to interpret the dream. Zizo declined saying he did not want to have a thing to do with the chief priest and that it was only but a dream and would never come to life.

"And if the dream does come to life, Zizo?" Tuna asked Zizo as he bathes in the water.

Zizo told him that it would never happen and that if it did happen, he would kill the baby before anyone does as such a baby without doubt will bring doom for the entire village.

"Do you know that this creature is always eating rotten foods whenever it wants to eat in my dream?" Zizo added, splashing water on himself.

"If he always does that, that means he is a **GHOULBRAHAM**, a creature that once perpetrated evil in the world because he was different from everyone. According to myth, the only thing that got him under control and eventually made him disappear was when they called him Ghoulbraham." Tuna told Zizo as he turns to come out of the stream.

He told Zizo that his father had once told him a story on Ghoulbraham when he was still very young. Placing his left hand on Zizo's shoulder, he prayed Zizo's dream does not become a reality. Both smiled at each other as they walked out of the stream.

It was evening, the sun was setting, and the birds were retiring to their nests. Tuna's dad sat on a chair at the middle of the compound fanning himself with a broad leaf as he watched his servants carrying out their duties. Tuna walked him wearing a tired face. He greeted his father but did not get a reply from him. Tuna moved closer to his father and then greeted him again. But his father did not reply him. Tuna turned to walk into his chamber when his father pulled him back and then gave him a hard knock on his chin, fallen him to the ground. In anger, he questioned Tuna asking him to tell him where he went to that made him not to respect the king's call. Tuna told him where he went to and this made his father angrier as he ordered him to go into his room before he would do something both of them would regret.

Tuna, holding the right side of his cheek, looked at his father and then walked out of him. Tuna could not eat his dinner as he was still in pains. His father got to know about this from one of his servants who wanted to clear away the foods that were served Zizo but discovered it was not torched by Tuna. His father followed into Tuna's room to inquire why he did not touch his meal. Tuna told him he could not eat as the right side of his face hurt. His father apologized over his outburst on Tuna, told him he did what he did because Zizo was covering his eyes, thus, making it impossible for him to know the position he Tuna was holding in the society. Tuna told his father that Zizo was a good friend and had never betrayed their friendship but always doing everything to make both of them happy.

"It is not good to keep company with someone who disrespects the king, Tuna." Tuna's dad said as he opened the plate-like structure that was on the table.

He told Tuna that he wants the best for Tuna, robbing Tuna's head with his right hand; he told Tuna that someday, he would understand all that he was doing for him and that he meant him good.

"I like this environment even though it looks strange. Everything about it is enchanting! But why haven't I seen this environment long before now? I know every nook and cranny of this village but never saw or been to this place. Wow! Without doubt, I believe this is where the gods reside. Let me go quickly to inform Tuna about this place so he too can behold the beauty of it." Zizo said as he admires the strange but beautiful environment.

Just as he turned to walk away, he heard the crying of a baby at the far end of the environment. He traced the voice to where it was coming from. Getting to the spot, he saw a handsome baby lying on one of the leaves that were on the ground.

"Who would have left such a beautiful baby in this lonely environment?" He moved closer to the baby as the baby cooed and then gave a nice smile.

Bending over to lift the baby up, the baby transformed into Ghoulbraham, but still did not stop smiling. Frightened Zizo, turned to run away but remembered the baby was alone in the environment and that no matter how beautiful the environment might be, there would be some dangerous animals lurking in the forest and the voice of the baby would attract them. He turned to lift Ghoulbraham from the leaf but did not see him again.

"Where has he gone to?" Zizo asked in surprise.

He looked around but did not see Ghoulbraham; he searched the environment but still did not see Ghoulbraham. And just as he called out **Ghoulbraham**, the enchanting environment turned into a messy environment with maggots coming from every tree that are in the environment. The weather became dark, so dark that Zizo could barely see himself. He tried calling out for help but could not as his tongue seems to have left his mouth. He struggled with all his might to call for help and just when he did, he woke up from his dream with sweat dripping from his body like someone who had just finished having his bathe... even though it was raining and the weather was cool.

"Thank the gods it was all a dream!" He sat on his bed and did not sleep again as he was scared he would have same dream or a dream that would be worse.

3

It was morning and the trees were waking up. Zizo came out of his house, carrying a seat. He walked to the famous tree that was behind his compound, and after staring at the tree, he dropped the seat he was holding and then sat on it under the tree.

"What is it you're thinking about Zizo with your hands under your chin, acting like the people that were before our generation?" Tuna asked Zizo as he walked into his compound wearing a smiling face.

Zizo stood up, walked into his room and then came out with a chair that was made from leaves. He gave the chair to Tuna as he resumed his sit. Tuna asked him why he was deep in thoughts and did not even notice him when he entered into his compound. Zizo tried sidelining it by asking Tuna to tell him what was discussed at the palace the day before that day. Tuna told him all his father told him about the cleansing. He congratulated Zizo for not agreeing to stay back the previous day, but went to farm to harvest his crops. He told Zizo that if he had not gone to the farm, he would have been in the same category with some of the lazy men in the village who have already started trooping into the king's palace to ask for food. Zizo, was caught up in thoughts again, as he wondered if the dream he had was connected to the cleansing, felling that the gods must be very angry with him. Tuna brought him back to himself by tapping his thigh. He asked Zizo why he was again deep in thoughts even when he was with him. Zizo gave a smile, saying he was just wondering how he would have been counted among the lazy inhabitants of the village. He tried asking Tuna another question so as to make him forget his intended question but failed as Tuna hush him down and then asked why he was sitting under his favorite tree and not wearing a smiling face as the tree was known by everyone in the village as his major source of happiness. Zizo looked at him with fearful eyes as he began narrating his dream to Tuna. Tuna listened, but felt every bit of the dream as if he was the one that dreamt it. Zizo cried as he ended his narration, saying he did not know who was after his life and that he did not want to die young without achieving all his dreams.

"Tuna, as I am now, I am scared of the dark; I mean, I am scared of sleeping because I will see him in my dream." Zizo said as he tried wiping the tears that were now racing on his face.

Tuna comforted him by saying Zizo was suffering from loneliness. He told Zizo that if he should get himself a wife, he would no longer be scared of sleeping and will always have someone that will share every of his worries with. Zizo gave a loud mocking laugh. He reminded Tuna that he was yet to get a wife and so cannot give advice on relationship issues. He told Tuna that he was not ready for marriage now as he already had a pressing issue in hand that he was trying to fix.

"You know what; I shall get for myself a wife the day you decide to get married." Zizo said, laughing and almost falling down from his seat.

Tuna soon started laughing making it seemed as if both of them were having a laughing competition.

"Wait a minute, both of us are of age and are doing well in our various lives. Most of the opposite sex in our village wishes to be married to us but we are not even looking at that direction. All we care about is going to farm and stream to bathe after getting our backs scotched by the sun…" Tuna said wiping off the joyful tears that were coming down his face as a result of the heavy laugh he had.

"Sincerely speaking, I see the passes the females in our village are making at me, including some of the married ones. But, like I earlier said, I have more important issues I want to fix as they are gradually becoming a threat to my existence." Zizo added as he rested his back on the tree.

Some weeks later, Tuna fell ill and could not accompany Zizo to farm. He was actually returning from Zizo's house when an unknown insect stung him on his neck, leaving him with severe aches all over his body. His father had called on the village chief priest to administer treatment to him and he was responding to the treatment. All the efforts made by Zizo to pay Tuna a visit so as to know how he was fairing was abortive as Tuna's father had ordered his servants never to allow him into the compound as he was the cause of Tuna's illness. Zizo went to the farm that day but did not harvest much as he was heartbroken because he was alone in the farm and was yet to know the state of Tuna's health. Wearing a long face, he journeyed to the stream. He was some meters away from the stream when he heard the strange female voice again singing and coming from the same direction, but this time around, there was a musical instrument that was played along with the song. He traced the sound to where it was coming from without looking downward or paying attention to what he was stepping on. Soon, he stepped on a quicksand and could not hold himself back again. He called out for help but help was nowhere near him. He cursed what made him left home and what made him decide to unravel the mystery behind the song that was coming out from the woods. He tried saying his last prayer but did not finish as the quicksand swallowed him up into a tunnel that was cool inside. Zizo imagined he was dead, but soon found himself staring at an opened field with woods around it. He became lost in thoughts as he imagined where on the planet he was.

"Ouch!" Zizo exclaimed in pain as he pinched himself to ascertain if truly he was still alive.

He robbed his eyes with the back of his palm, and then used his eyes to comb the field but did not see anyone and did not hear the voice again. Still wondering what would have happened, he felt a touch on his left shoulder. He turned around and saw a skinny beautiful female holding a flute in her left hand.

"Who are you"? Zizo asked as he uses his eyes to scan the lady.

"I should be the one asking you because you are the one that walked into my domain. Who are you?" The lady asked Zizo as she walked to sit on a fallen tree that was closed by.

Zizo told her who he was and where he was from. He asked the lady to do same as he took his sit beside her. The lady told Zizo who she was. She told him she was from Zizo's village, but was banished from the village because her family was inflicted with a disease by the chief priest of the village as a result of her father not allowing him to take the only piece of land that her family had.

"Why didn't your family report the chief priest to the king?" Zizo asked with his eyes blood red.

She told Zizo that they did not tell the king because he and the village chief priest were best of friends and are wolves in sheep clothing. Zizo was amazed upon hearing that King Katinu was not the only warrior that survived the war between their village and the other village, but that through the magical powers of the chief priest, King Katinu killed the other survivals. He stared at the lady whose name was **GAYU** for some minutes, then asked to see her parents. The beautiful Gayu broke down in tears and then told Zizo that her parents were dead as a result of the disease that was inflicted on them. She told him that her being alive was still a mystery to her. She told him that she had no one to play with or talk to except the trees and leaves in the forest and that was why she always came out to sing to them. Just as Zizo was trying to console her, a teardrop escaped from his right eye. He cleaned it quickly and then asked Gayu to please take him to her house so he would be visiting her often. She declined request saying Zizo's knowing her place would bring doom upon her. Zizo down on his knees, begged her to show him her place, assuring her that as long as he lived, no harm would come near her. Taking Zizo by his right hand, she took him deep into the tall trees that were in front of the field. Zizo saw a small but beautiful house in the forest. He admired the beautiful flowers around the house that added beauty to Gayu's house and never remembered the field he met Gayu was the same field he had seen in his dream, the dream he could not speak, and did not remember that the beautiful flowers were the same flowers that turned rotten.

"Wow! Small abode, yes, beautiful, yes, do I like it here? Yes", Zizo soliloquized as he walked around the house with Gayu following from behind.

"Now that you've known my house, can you now return to your village before night falls?" Gayu asked.

Zizo begged to spend some minutes in the environment but Gayu refused, saying she wished to be alone. Zizo refused to leave. He sat on the grasses in front of the house, saying he would not leave unless Gayu promised she would allow him visit her the following day. She agreed but warned Zizo not to tell anyone about her. He smiled and then crossed his chest with his hands, promising Gayu he would not tell anyone about her. She allowed Zizo to hold her left hand as they journeyed out of the environment.

***

It was evening, smiling Zizo whistled down the path that led to his house, holding a fishing line that held three fishes, dangling on the line. On his head was a basket with the little crops he had harvested. Some ladies coming from the opposite direction offered to help him but he declined, saying what he was carrying were not heavy. The ladies insisted in carrying the items from him and after discovering they would not go unless he granted their requests, he granted them their request. He watched them in admiration as they took the items from him and then walking ahead of him. He was still admiring their charisma when the sight of Gayu flashed through his mind.

"She is a beauty to behold. She is brave too. Living in that lonely but lovely place for only the Mother Nature knows how long is not easy. I must try and see her tomorrow so she will tell me more about herself." Zizo said as he started walking behind the ladies.

As the ladies walked, they chatted on who would marry Zizo and how lucky she would be. The one-time lovely chat between the ladies soon turned into a disagreement as no one of them wanted the other to have him to herself.

At Zizo's compound, the ladies dropped the items in front of his house, all faking smiles. Zizo thanked them for their kind heart and that he was going to handsomely repay them someday. He barely had finished talking when one of the ladies spoke up, saying the only kind thing she would want Zizo to pay her with is him agreeing to marry her. At this, her other friends turned and looked at her in surprise and hate. Zizo, who was about going into his room, turned back and after looking at the lady that spoke, gave her a smile.

"No doubt you are beautiful and have good character. I have also been seeing you around and I can tell that you are hard working. Your type is one that every man in the village would want to have as a partner. However, I am not ready to settle down soon. When I am, I will let you know." He gave her a smile and taking a short glimpse on the other ladies, smiled and walked into his house.

The other ladies fired harsh words at the lady that spoke, accusing her of wanting to take what was rightfully theirs. Her voice was no match to theirs and when she sensed the anger that was in the tone of their voices, she ran out of the compound. Her calculation was correct as the ladies ran after her.

Later in the evening, Zizo again tried visiting Tuna to see him and have an update on his health. Like before, the servants in the compound did not allow him into the compound. He begged them to at least tell him how Tuna was fairing but his plead were ignored as none of them gave him the answer he sought. They had been instructed not to tell a thing to Zizo. Zizo bowing his head, walked away. He soon got home but sadness took every bit of his heart. He went and sat under the tree behind his house, thinking it would make him happy but, no, it did not as he was alone and needed to share some of his heart feelings with Tuna. He needed Tuna's advice on the incident that happened at his house, and the strange lady he saw in a strange environment. He wished Tuna would just pop out from the thin air and give him listening ears. Still deep in thoughts, he looked up and saw that the moon coming out of its hiding place in the cloud.

"What if I try spending the night at Gayu's place?" Zizo soliloquized.

After some minutes, he got up, walked into the room and then came out wearing a different cloth.

"I just hope she does not get angry and then chase me out in the dark." Zizo soliloquized again to himself as he walked out of his house.

He trekked on the narrow pathway that led to the stream, whistling a rhythm that was known only to him with a smile he had not worn on his face since he was born. Getting close to the stream, he stopped whistling. He placed his right hand behind his right ear as if there was a sound that was coming out from the bush.

"What am I doing, listening to no sound in the dark? She has really gotten a hold on me." Zizo said to himself as he turned and then took the path that led to the open field.

He saw the quicksand, but this time around, gladly stepped on it. He folded his arms across his chest as the tunnel took him to the open field. Getting to the open field, he discovered the place was more beautiful at night than it was during the day. He saw fireflies lightening up the field as they fly in different directions as if they were going for a night party, while some of them were returning to put the house in order. He saw some other glowing tiny insects sitting on the flowers of all the trees in the field, adding beauty to the field.

"Wow!" I never knew there is a place like this in this world." Said Zizo with his hands placed on his waist.

Zizo was still admiring the beauty of the environment when he heard someone call his name. He turned around and saw Gayu walking towards him, still holding her flute, looking so amazing in the night. He marveled at her beauty.

"What are you doing here? Why come here to disturb the peace of the night?" Gayu asked as she stood in front of Zizo.

Zizo looked around, wondering how he was disturbing the peace of the peace. Visiting the field without Gayu's permission was understandable, but disturbing the peace of the night was a mystery to him. Not wanting to be kicked out by Gayu, as he was scared of the dark, he apologized to her, telling her it was not intentional. He told her he needed someone to talk to and his best friend who always gave him listening ears was sick and he did not know his present condition.

"So, are these the reason why you came uninvited?" Gayu asked as she moved around Zizo who was by now frightened.

Zizo answered her yes, and that he was also scared of a particular dream he would like to keep to himself until the time was ripe for him. He begged Gayu to allow him pass the night in the field, so he would not have to be a pest to her. Gayu picked up a firefly. She placed it on her arm with her eyes fixed on Zizo. After some minutes, she asked him to follow her and they both walked into one of the parts that separated the trees with Zizo always turning back to get a glimpse of the beautiful field and the creatures that were displaying their awesomeness. At Gayu's place, Zizo realized the beauty in the field was nothing compelled to the beauty of Gayu's abode.

"Can you come in?" Gayu asked Zizo as he admired the surrounding. Zizo came back to his senses and then joined Gayu at the entrance of her house.

4

"It's morning," Gayu said to sleeping Zizo as she tapped him to wake up.

Zizo cleaned his eyes as he woke up from his sleep. Zizo looked throw the window and saw that it was already morning and the birds have started singing.

"I slept! I did not wake up at night!" Zizo said as he jumped in excitement.

Gayu watched him in surprise, as she did not understand what Zizo was saying. He turned around and after exchanging pleasantries with Gayu, ran outside to see if the fireflies and shining creatures were still there but they were not.

He turned around and stared at Gayu.

"The beauty of last night was awesome! I mean, is it always like that here?" Smiling Zizo asked Gayu.

Gayu told him that the previous night was nothing compared to other nights. She told him that it was one of the reasons she had not die of loneliness in the forest.

"You see, those things you saw last night were not here when my family and I first moved into this forest. When we first moved into this forest, there was no light anywhere and no beauty at all in the forest until one evening when my mother and I were returning from the field, a snake bit her. She was in terrible pains and at the point of death when she requested I sing for her a song, her favorite song. As a last wish, I sang her a song, and just as I started blowing my flute to add to the song, I saw fireflies and the tiny shining creatures coming out from the woods, all-shining brightly as they gather around my dying mother. Some of them perched on her ankle, where she was bitten. I really did not know what they were doing until my mother whose eyes were already closed, opened them and with a smiling face, told me she felt a relieved from the aches she was suffering from. She thanked me for the song and then gave up the ghost." Gayu said wearing a look that would make one wonder if she was happy or sad.

"Were they actually trying to save her?" Zizo asked Gayu giving her all his attention.

"I think so because after the death of my mother, there was no such thing as snake or any wild animal in these woods, guess they also chased them out as well. And that night was the last dark night in the woods." Gayu concluded, now letting a smile show on her face.

Zizo asked the whereabouts of her father when all these happened. She told him that her father did not last a month after they left the village for the woods. Zizo held her close to console her. He told her he believed her parents were in heaven constantly watching over her. He encouraged her never to feel alone as he would be coming on daily bases to check on her. Gayu lifted up her head to look at Zizo's blue eyes that were now shining brightly in excitement. Though Zizo wanted to be keeping her company on daily basis, he was not specific on the hour of the day he would be coming because he did not see Ghoulbraham in his dream and wanted to be sure, if sleeping in the woods will keep him away from seeing Ghaoulbraham in his dream. Gayu smiled and then thanked him for his kind heart. She asked him what his plans were for the day. Zizo sensing he had got for himself a new friend told her his plans for the day and that he would want to start going to be able to do some works on his farm.

"Can that wait because I wish to show you around the woods... that is if you do not mind." Smiling Gayu asked Zizo as she releases herself from Zizo's grip.

Without giving it a second thought, Zizo agreed to her request.

"Thank you!" Gayu said to Zizo as she held his right hand and then led him out of the compound.

She took him to another quarter of the woods, one that made Zizo wonder if the place was finer than the field where he met Gayu. In this new place was a fountain that had shining waters with trees that have different colors of leaves and fruits. Something that looks like the moon shines up in the sky. There was absolutely nothing like heat in this environment. Zizo was very sure that the gods even though he did not believe in them, live in woods and that where he was standing on could be the place where they take their bathe. Just as Zizo was still admiring the environment, when a colorful parrot flew and perched on his shoulder, another came rested on Gayu's shoulder.

"This is home!" Zizo exclaimed still admiring the environment.

It was already afternoon and the scotching sun was shining up in the sky with the people of Inoko hurriedly going about their various duties. Zizo walked down a part thinking of his experience in the company of Gayu. He wondered if there are actually females in the world that would be so fun to be with. Just as he wondered, he stumbled upon one of the ladies that helped him out the other day with his fishes and farming implements. In fact, it was the one that wished he married her that he stumbles on.

"Hi!" Said the lady wearing a stunning smile on her face.

"Hi! how are you doing today?" Zizo asked her, wishing he never came across her that day.

She told him that she had gone to his farm to look for him but did not see him there, waited at his house for many hours but did not see him. That as a matter of fact, she was actually coming from his house. Zizo asked her if she was okay, as she had never done those before. She told him yes, but that she missed him and needed to talk to him about some things. Zizo was shocked upon hearing this. He asked her to tell him, what exactly she wanted to see him for, but she insisted the issue be discussed at Zizo's place. Not wanting to cause a scene, he asked her to follow him to his house so she would tell him all she had to tell him. Zizo was shocked at the way his compound looked. There was not a single leaf on the ground. Everything seemed to be in their right places.

"Surprise?" The lady asked as she gets Zizo a seat to sit on.

Standing in front of Zizo, she asked if she should tell him what she had to tell him. Zizo hushed her as she was about starting; he stood up from his seat and then offered it to the lady to sit on.

"It is better you sit for me to stand while you tell me what you want to tell me, than for me to sit and listen to you, a visitor standing while I am sitting down." Zizo said as he put her on the seat.

At this, the lady gave a sigh and then let out a smile on her face. She told Zizo how she had swept the compound, made him food and went looking for him. Zizo thanked her but insisted on knowing why she did them.

"Are you still a kid?" The lady asked in disgust.

"Off course I did all these things because I love you Zizo." She said staring into Zizo's eyes as if to bring out words from his mouth.

Zizo smiled at her. He smiled at her and after some seconds of silence, told her he was going to think about it and will get back to her in no time. His words were comforting to her as she offered to serve Zizo his meal, which he politely declined. He allowed her some minutes in his house before seeing her off.

The lady walked towards her house, feeling hopeful that her love will soon be appreciated by Zizo. She smiled and greeted everyone that she came across. Just as she got close to her house, she saw a figure that looked like that of a human, covered in a dark cloth from his head to toe. However, the figure was not looking at her, but her house. She paused and wondered who was behind the clothing. After some seconds of standing and wondering who it was, she summoned courage and then walked up to the creature.

"Who are you and what are you doing in my house?" The lady asked the figure.

"Who I am does not matter now, what matters is that you desist from that thing you are trying to do." The figure answered the lady without turning back.

He warned her that if she does not give up on what she was doing, she would not live to tell what would happen at the end of the journey. His words did not frighten the lady, it instead made her asks him to leave his house that minute, and never come back.

"I need his combination and that of a lady I have already chosen so as to become me." The figure spoke again as he turns around to reveal his identity to the lady.

"Now you want to show me your..." The lady gave an abrupt stop as she saw the figures face, Ghoulbraham.

She screamed and ran out of her compound, calling on villagers to come to her rescue. Her call for help was quickly heard as some of the brave men and women of the village came to her rescue. They followed her to her house, combed the house and its environment but did not see anyone. Ghoulbraham, the green creature with three eyes had disappeared into thin hair. She was asked by her rescuers to narrate what she saw and she did. All of them were confused about the description, as they had never heard of such in their life. The eldest amongst them, suggested they see the chief priest of the land as he is in the best position to unravel the mystery behind the incident.

She begged them to accompany her to the chief priest's abode, as it was a sacrilege for a lady to visit the chief priest alone.

***

It was still in the afternoon and the sun was still shining brightly in the sky. The chief priest was inside his hut muttering some words that could be heard only by him. Carcasses of different creatures lay about on the roof of the hut, which differentiated the hut from every other hut in the village. He came out of the hut upon seeing his village people walking towards the hut.

"What brought the people of our village to my hut this afternoon when the gods are having their meeting?" The chief priest asked as he gets hold his staff that was lying on the wall of his hut.

"Good the gods are having their meeting. It will do just fine if you relate what we have to tell you to them so they will give us quick reply." One of the people spoke out.

The chief priest gave a disturbing look as no one in the village had ever spoken to him in that manner. He asked them what happened and the lady who Ghoulbraham had appeared to narrate her ordeal to him. He asked for the description of what visited her and upon hearing it, he became uneasy. He looked around in fright and then asked the people give him some minutes to consult the gods of the land, which the people gladly gave their consent, all-wondering why the chief priest was uneasy. The chief priest hurriedly walked into his hurt. He sat down with his legs folded like that of a monk that is meditating. He muttered some words and although his words were heard by all that was present in his compound, none understood what he was saying as according to them, he was speaking the language of the spirit. Minutes later, the chief priest came out of his hurt wearing a more confusing and frightened look. He asked the people to return home, as the gods were silent on the issue. He asked the lady to return to her house assuring her that nothing would happen to her so long she does not rush into doing whatever she started recently. Though she did not understand the meaning of what he said, she could not ask further questions as according to the chief priest, the gods were silent about the issue.

"Let your ears be on the ground as you all will be hearing from King Katinu soonest on this issue." The chief priest told them as they all walked out of his compound in their twos and threes with the maiden wondering what the creature was and what it meant by desist from what you are about starting.

"The one that was dreaded by all is about coming back to life! King Katinu must hear this." The chief priest said as he rushed back into his hurt.

"I still find it hard to believe that Zizo would stay many days without checking on me to know how I am faring, even after knowing I am actually down in health as a result of the sting I got while I was returning from his place." Tuna exclaimed as he manages to sit up on what he was laying on.

"I told you before but you would not listen. That Zizo you call your friend, does not wish you well. In fact, I am beginning to think he has a hand in the insect that bit you." Tuna's dad said as he helped Tuna rests his back on a wall.

"Surprised Zizo has not visited me yet, but I am very sure he has no hands in what happened to me dad. It was just a mere coincidence." Tuna said as he looked away.

"If you cannot learn now, I mean know the people that truly love you, when then are you going to start learning? I have some things to attend to at the palace, will talk to you when I return." Said Tuna's dad as he gets up and walks away, asking a male servant to attend to Tuna.

Tuna turned to see which of the servant was asked to take care of him. He saw that it was his favorite servant, the one that never lied to him. Using his right hand, he beckoned on the servant to come closer to him.

"Is it true Zizo has been coming to check on how I am doing, but never allowed in?" Tuna stylishly asked the servant so he would easily get the answer he sought.

The servant bowed his head for some seconds... raising it up, he answered him 'no.'

He told Tuna that Zizo never came looking for him.

He told him there was a day he saw him on the road, but Zizo acted like he did not know him... even when he called Zizo's name. Tuna was shocked to the marrow upon hearing this. He asked the servant to let him be, as he needed some minutes to think. The servant bowed and then left Tuna to himself. Tuna wondered why Zizo would do such a thing to him, why he would let him die and never bothered looking back. He bit his lips and prayed he gets back on his feet on time so he would confront with tears coming down from his eyes, he remembered the good old times he had with Zizo... he wished all he was hearing were not true.

5

It was already evening and the big red sun was beginning to set in the village of Inoko. Zizo packed everything he had outside into his house. He brought out a basket which he had put a sumptuous meal for Gayu. He smiled, as he smells the nice aroma that was coming from the basket.

"I know Gayu will be happier today because of this meal I took my time to prepare." Zizo smiled as he spoke aloud to himself.

"Time to go where those fireflies and shining creatures come from, and to know if staying in Gayu's house keeps Ghoulbraham away." He added as he walked out of the house.

He smiled at everyone he saw on the road as he threaded the path that led to the stream. Some people asked where he was going with a basket of food. Zizo answered he was going for an evening fishing and needed to eat something before fishing. He was so happy because no one asked where his fishing tools that he was to use in fishing were. When he got to the stream, he looked around to see if someone was around. After looking around for some seconds and satisfied no one was around, he hurriedly walked into the path that led to the beautiful field where he met Gayu. Like Gayu was waiting for him at the other side of the tunnel. She gave Zizo a hug that was accompanied with a smiling face. Zizo was shocked, as she had never done that to him. He asked her if she was okay with what she did; she gave a positive reply with a nod of her head.

"Come let us go to up to the fountain and watch." Gayu could not finish her statement as Zizo knelt in front of her, asking she take him to the place where the fireflies and shining creatures come out from.

"But that is what I want to show you Zizo." Gayu said again with a smiling face.

Zizo did not understand what she meant. And as if she could read his mind, she told him that the fountain was where the fireflies and shinning creatures come out from. The news struck Zizo's heart that he could not help but attempted to lift Gayu up. To Zizo, it was the best news he had ever received.

"Let us go now before you miss their beautiful coming out." Zizo gave Gayu his left hand as he allowed her take him to the fountain with shinning waters, the place he believed was where the gods live.

She offered Zizo a seat that was made from shining stones and then sat beside him but on the green grass that covered the ground of the environment. Zizo liked everything he saw but was uneasy as he waited patiently for the hour when he would see what he craved for. Minutes later and it seemed like nothing was going to happen. He turned to look at Gayu. Just as he was about asking when the fireflies would come, Gayu shushed him by pointing at the shinning ball like thing that looked like a moon. He turned and looked at what she was pointing at and could not believe what he saw happening. He saw colorful fireflies trooping out from the moon-like thing, all flashing their lights as they trooped out.

"Just when I thought I have seen it all, I discover I have not seen anything at all." Zizo said to himself as he washed in amazement.

As soon as there were no more fireflies in the moon-like figure, the shinning creatures started coming out in circles. Zizo washed with his mouth wide opened.

"Are these not what you wanted to see?" Gayu asked Zizo without looking at him.

Zizo answered him yes, but that what he saw just made him know that he had seen even more than what he planned seeing. Gayu smiled.

"You may not have seen it all you know!" She added.

"So tell me, how has your village being?" She asked.

Zizo gave a loud laugh. "You mean our village?" He asked.

"The village is no longer my village, not after what they did to me and my family." Gayu said now changing her countenance.

Zizo said he still wondered when all Gayu told him happened as he could not remember it.

"It is not that I doubt you Gayu, it is just that the people living in the village are now very peaceful and loving, they look like people who would never do such a thing to someone." He concluded.

Gayu gave a sigh, and then asked Zizo to tell her all that has been happening in the village. Still admiring the sight of the fireflies, Zizo told her the recent happening in the village. He told her how one of the maidens of the village had seen a strange being in her compound and when she and the people that came to her rescue visited the hut of the chief priest, the chief priest did not give them any cogent answer or solution to what had happened to her. He instead asked them to return to their various homes, but keep their ears to the ground, as the king would be summoning them on the issue. Zizo concluded by saying that everyone in the community is now careful with his or her life. Gayu asked the name of the creature the maiden saw at her compound. Zizo told her he was not there when it happened and so was not sure of what she saw in her house.

"You know what? If the village becomes so unbearable for people to live in, I'll just take from my belongings, the ones that are very important to me and then relocate to your environment." Zizo said with a smiling face.

"Or will you not welcome me?" Zizo asked her and she gave a chuckle while shaking her head in disagreement to what Zizo asked.

Zizo placed his hand on hers as they both watched the enchanting movements of the fireflies and the shining creatures. Zizo pulled Gayu's right hand as he led her to the open fields so he would see how the shining creatures settle on the trees.

"When are you going to visit me in Inoko"? Zizo asked staring into Gayu's eyes.

***

It was morning and the servants in Tuna's compound were busying themselves with their various duties. Tuna too was trying to fix his bed when his father walked into his room. After the exchange of greeting between him and his father, was asked to sit by his father, as there was an important thing he wanted to discuss with him.

"Dad, I hope it is not about Zizo you want to bug me with me with this early in the morning as I have better things to worry my head about." Tuna asked as he took his sit.

His father smiled and then gave a sigh.

"Before now, you used to hang out with your friend Zizo, do not know if he is still a friend of yours." His father said looking into Tuna's eyes as if to get something out of them.

"So, it is about Zizo after all!" Tuna asked in anger as he tried standing up to take his leave.

His father calmed him down by telling him it is not about Zizo but about him. He also asked Tuna allows him finish what he had to tell him before he would take a leave.

"Like I was saying, you used to hang around him but not anymore after the questionable attitude he showed you." He cleared his throat as he continued. "You see, I will not always be here for you when you need someone to talk to or to share your worries with. What I want you to do is to get for yourself, a lady you will marry and build a family with. I have always waited for you to take this bold step and after seeing you are not ready to take it, or should I say it did not come to your mind, I decided to have this meeting with you. I hope you understand I mean well for you." He concluded with his hands between his thighs.

Tuna thanked him for taking out time to tell him what he should have long done. He apologized for not ever carrying out his father's biddings and then promised to do just as he had advised him. These statements sank deep into his father's ears as he smiled.

"I have always known that this day will come, but I did not know it would come this soon." Said Tuna's father as he gave Tuna a pat on his shoulder. "I hope the gods bless you with a good lady" He said as he turned to walk out of the room but was met with one of his servants who told him that the King's messenger just left, saying that the king wants everyone to be at his palace right away.

"What would have made the king call for an emergency meeting at this hour of the day?" He wondered.

King Katinu's message soon spread like raging fire round the village as everyone was seen at his palace few minutes after he sent his messenger out to the people. It was as if they were waiting for his call. None in attendance bothered him or herself to sit except Tuna's dad. None even hailed King Katinu as he stepped out to address the people; not because the incident that happened the previous day made them not to hail him, but because King Katinu was not wearing smile on his face. Even the chief priest that followed him from behind was not smiling as well. They murmured amongst themselves wondering if it was the situation at hand was the reason for their frowning faces.

"People of Inoko," King Katinu spoke as he cleared his throat. "It is no longer news that something strange happened in our community yesterday afternoon, something that gave me sleepless night."

His words made his people more confused and frightened at the same time. As if to allow what he had said, King Katinu allowed the people to murmur for some seconds before speaking again. He told them that the strange being that was seen at a maiden's house the previous day was a creature that once hunted the community many years ago, during the days of their fore fathers. He told them that the creature does not just come out from wherever his abode might be, but comes out when something evil has happened or was about to happen. Every of king's Katinu's words struck the people's heart like a pin, however, what really got them more scared was when King Katinu told them that what the maiden saw the previous day was the ghost of the creature and not the creature itself, which means that the creature is already in the village.

"What did the gods advice we do in this situation?" An elder spoke from the crowd.

King Katinu did not respond to the question, however, gave the chief priest the opportunity to answer the question. The chief priest took his position beside king Katinu as he spoke to the people. He told them that the gods have spoken; their words are final because their ways are straight. He told them the gods have promised to do something about the dreadful creature but that they should all observe the traditions of the community and never compromise them no matter what. Like a spell was casted on them, the words of the chief priest sank into the hearts of the people and they all jumped in jubilation because the gods have promised to do something about it.

Zizo and Gayu arrived Zizo's compound with Zizo leading the way. All through their journey from the woods to Zizo's house, Gayu never said a thing. She kept mute as she watched everything that came to her sight. Zizo never bothered asking her any questions, he just allowed her to feel her eyes as it had been very long she last saw the village. When she got to Zizo's house, she was amazed at the way his house appeared, as it was better than all the houses she saw on their way.

"You have a nice house, Zizo!" She spoke as she sat on the seat Zizo offered her.

"Sorry the seat is not as beautiful as the once in your environment" Zizo said as he too took his sit in front of Gayu.

Gayu asked him if the village was usually that quiet and empty. She asked because she did not see anyone all through their journey and there was no sound of any kind from anywhere. Zizo told her that the village was not a noisy one, but was surprise at what was happening.

"I guess the King Katinu has summoned everyone to his palace because it is the only thing that will ever make the village this calm." Zizo said as he looked around to see if he would see someone.

"I should be on my way home now, don't want someone to see me here" Gayu spoke as standing up from her seat.

"But you just came?" Zizo spoke with a shaking voice.

"I know I just came, but I need to go now because my body wants me to leave now." Zizo was heartbroken at her reply.

He asked her if the house was not good enough for her, or if he had unknowingly upset her. Placing her both hands on Zizo's cheeks, Gayu promised to visit him again at his request. Her words gave him solace as he let out a smile on his face.

"I hope you spend more time when next you visit" Zizo said still maintaining the smile on his face.

Gayu nodded in agreement. She stretched out her left hand to Zizo as she allowed him lead her out of the house. They walked smiling and chatting on how their next meeting would be. Getting some meters away from the stream, Zizo waved goodbye to Gayu as she journeyed on. He did not know that Tuna was in the stream. He turned his back and journeyed home.

"Hi" Said Tuna to Gayu as Gayu was close to the path that led to her world.

She turned and looked at Tuna, then greeted him. Tuna asked for her name but she refused telling him. And when he asked to know her, she said some other time, telling him that she was in a hurry to get a particular leaf that is at the stream, a leaf that two eyes must not see when it is being plucked. She asked Tuna for his name and his village. Tuna smiled and gave her the answers, waiting for more questions, which never came as Gayu asked to be left alone, promising she would visit him the following day. Tuna was delighted. He granted her request and then leapt out of her sight in excitement. Gayu waited for some seconds for Tuna to be out of sight before taking the path that led to her world. Leaping Tuna soon met Zizo on the road. Upon seeing him, he tried dodging Zizo but could not as Zizo too had seen him. He called out to Tuna as he ran to meet him.

"Hi! Thank goodness you are well!" Zizo said as he ran his eyes on Tuna's body.

"See, I am not ready for you this afternoon. I have some important matters I want to attend to now, will see you tomorrow." Tuna said and then walked out on Zizo without giving him any room for talks.

Zizo watched in amazement, wondering what must have happened to his friend.

"Well, he said he would be coming to my place tomorrow, I will just wait for him to come so he will tell me what is wrong with him." Zizo soliloquized and then continued his journey home.

Tuna rushed into his compound and then into his room carrying in his heart, a mixed feeling. He wondered if he had fallen in love with Gayu, what exactly did she need the leaf for, what made him see Zizo, if Zizo had seen Gayu, and if all he heard about Zizo are true. He sat on his bed with his hands behind his ears.

"I have already told him I will be visiting him tomorrow; I will visit him. If not for anything, at least to question him on why he never checked on him during his ill days." He was still speaking aloud when his father walked into his room, wearing a worried look.

He asked his father why he was wearing the look and he narrated all that the king and chief priest told them at the palace.

"Although the chief priest assured us that the gods are going to take care of this strange creature, I just do not believe him because of the way he spoke... he spoke like he was not sure of what he was saying and the eyes of King Katinu was fool of sorrows." Tuna's father said, taking a sit in front of Tuna.

Tuna told his father to cheer up and believe the words of the chief priest as he was the closest to the gods and had never failed them in his communication with the gods.

"I hope the gods do because the creature whose description fits that of Ghoulbraham is a no mercy creature that would have dealt with everyone before the gods would do something about him." He said almost in tears.

Tuna reminded his father the story he had told him about the creature, how it was sent back to where it came from by the mentioning of his name, Ghoul. His father looked at him with the tears now coming down from his eyes. He told Tuna that the story was true, but did not know the name the creature was with now as history had it that the creature usually changed his name, or add to his name whenever it is been reborn. That it did this so no one could send him back.

"Well, let us keep our fingers crossed, trusting on the gods." Tuna said to his dad as he stood up and then walked out of the room, thinking about Gayu.

Later that night while Tuna slept, he dreamt of himself been tied to a tree with bloody marks all over his body. He cried in pain, he tried calling for help but discovered he could not as his tongue was on the ground staring at him. It had been cut off by the unknown being that tied him down. He wept like a baby, knowing there was no escape for him. He bowed his head in pain. Just then, he heard footsteps and hurriedly raised his head to see whom. Before him was Ghoulbraham holding a whip in his right hand, and a rotten meat that looks like that of the head of an unknown animal in his left hand. Tuna was frightened to his spine, could not control himself from wetting his pant. Ghoulbraham took a bite from the meat on his left hand. As he chewed it, he allowed saliva to drop from his mouth.

"I visited and the message was passed to everyone, but not to you as you were busy doing what you should not even do... trying to create a bond that will delay my coming, a bond that you will not live to see its end." Ghoulbraham said as he used the whip on Tuna. "I will let you go now but will not if you go on with what you plan to start... if you do, your head will be next in my left hand." He gave out a wicked laugh and then walked out.

Tuna woke up from his sleep, frightened, yet wondered what the dreamt meant. Meanwhile, Zizo slept peacefully in his house on his leafy bed that was once his father's. He dreamt of Gayu running in the compound giving out a smile that revealed her teeth. It was the best dream Zizo ever had after the death of his parents.

6

It was morning, Zizo was not thinking of going to his farm to cultivate it, but thinking of how he would visit Gayu in her world. Since Zizo met Gayu, he barely went to his farm. He would instead visit Gayu and watched the fascinating environment that oftentimes made me forget eating. He was about locking the door when he sensed something moved passed him to the rear of his house. He left the door and then slowly moved to the rear of his house. For a second he thought it was Ghoulbraham he saw resting its back against the tree where he usually sat until he walked closer to the tree and discovered there was nothing there. He turned and to his surprise, he saw Gayu standing in front of him.

"Hi, I was about leaving for your place" Zizo said stuttering in excitement.

"Well, there will be no need for that because I am already here. I thought I would see you yesterday night but you did not come." Gayu asked Zizo looking into his eyes.

Zizo told her that he did not come because he wanted to be sure of something. He held Gayu's hand and then led her to the frontage of his house; there he gave her a seat to sit on. Holding Gayu's hands, he told her about the dreams on Ghoulbraham he had been having but had stopped having it since the day he met her. He told Gayu as she listened in surprise. He told her that her coming into his life had really changed everything about him, including his dream. He went down on his knees and then asked for Gayu's hands in marriage.

"You want this, but did not come to me to tell me!" Gayu asked Zizo.

Zizo apologized to her, said he was actually coming to her place to do it in the environment he cherished most. His words made Gayu happy as she asked him to follow her to the environment. Zizo was happy, but asked she stayed with him until evening when the fireflies and shinning creatures will be out; that he would want them to be a witness to whatever he would tell her. She smiled and gave Zizo a hug. They were still hugging when Tuna walked in and saw them in each other's arms.

"What is going on here?" Tuna asked as he walked closer to them.

Zizo, still holding Gayu in his arms, welcomed Tuna. He introduced Gayu to Tuna and then told Tuna that she was the one he wished to settle down with. Zizo's heart was pierced by his words as he had intended to see Gayu soon even though he did not know when, he felt there was a connection between him and her.

"I know you are a betrayal, but I did not know that your betrayal has increased to this level. Why would you betray our friendship this way?" Tuna asked in pain.

Zizo told him he did not understand what Tuna was saying. Tuna told him how he was ill for a couple of days and he did not he did not bother coming to see him; the lady he intended settling down with had now been taken by him. Tuna walked out without giving Zizo any room for explanation. Gayu asked Zizo the meaning of what Tuna meant when he said Zizo did not pay him a visit when he was sick. Zizo too asked Gayu what Tuna meant when he said he was planning to settle down with her. Neither Gayu nor Zizo could answer the question their questions. Like a spark of fire, they remembered what they were about doing before Tuna came in. Zizo locked the knob of his door, holding Gayu by the hand; he led her out of his house.

Tuna got home, paced around the compound in anger like a raging lion that is about to attack a prey. He was still pacing around the compound when his father walked in.

"What is going on here, son?" His father asked Tuna.

Tuna narrated what he saw at Zizo's place. He told his father that Gayu was the person he intended marrying. Tuna's dad laughed at him, saying he warned Tuna about his friendship with Zizo but he did not listen. He advised him to pick up the pieces of his life and move on, as it is the only thing he could do.

"No dad, it is not the only thing I can do no. and if it the only thing I can do now, I definitely will pay Zizo back in his own coin someday." Tuna spoke in anger and then walked into his room.

He vowed never to have a thing to do with Zizo ever again.

***

It was evening, the fireflies and shining creatures were already flying out of the moonlike object that stood still in the sky that covered the environment where the fountain with shining waters was... Zizo and Gayu sat on the field, watching them as they flew out of it. Ghoulbraham appeared behind Zizo and Gayu but they did not see him as they were both engrossed in what was about to happen

"This is the moment I have been waiting for. Now that it is here, I ask you please be mine." Zizo told Gayu, holding her hands as he stared into her eyes.

"Well, I do not want to be yours, I would not have visited you, would not have showed you this place we are now because it is intend the place of the gods, the place where I buried my parents. I want to spend the rest of my life with you, but please promise never to make me cry or turn down any request you know will make me happy." Gayu spoke in under her breathe but Zizo heard her words.

Zizo promised to do her wills and promised to stay with her until her dying day.

"SO SHALL IT BE." Ghoulbraham said and then vanished before they could look back.

Zizo asked Gayu if she was the one that spoke, but she replied she did not speak, but was wondering if it was Zizo that made the statement. Like Gayu, Zizo said he was not the one that spoke.

"Guess the gods are in support of our union." Zizo said with a smiling face.

Every day became a blessed day for Gayu and Zizo as they cherished each other's company and could not do a day without seeing each other. It was so great that Gayu decided to be staying with Zizo, visiting her enchanting world once in a blue moon. On the other end, the village was now peaceful as everyone went about his or her duties without getting to see any strange being. However, Tuna and the lady who worked for Zizo and wished he married her were not happy. The lady was angry with Gayu for taking her man, while Tuna was angry with Zizo for taking the girl of his dream from him. So, one day while the lady was returning from where she went visiting a friend, she saw Tuna resting his back on a tree. She greeted and when she was about walking passed him, Tuna stopped her.

"Why are you faking the smile on your face when things are not okay with you?" Tuna said as he moved away from the tree to where the lady was standing.

The lady told him she did not know what he was talking about.

"I know how you tried getting to be Zizo's wife by helping do all his house chores, and how instead of marrying you, brought home a strange woman, a woman I actually saw first and was planning to marry before he snatched her away from me." Tuna said bowing his head.

"So, what do you want us to do now?" The lady asked.

Tuna said he carried out a research on the woman and found out that her family was banished from the village because of the atrocity they perpetrated in the village.

"The king does not know she is in this community, so I suggest we inform him about her. Are you thinking what I am thinking?" Tuna asked the lady with an evil smile on his face.

The lady thought for some second as if to figure out what he was saying. And when she did, she too gave a wicked smile and then asked they see King Katinu right away. They walked hurriedly not knowing that Ghoulbraham was following them from behind.

King Katinu was having a meeting with the chief priest when Tuna and the lady entered and greeted them.

"I smell something," The chief priest said and then used his nose to sniff around the palace.

"What brought you to my palace?" King Katinu asked as he settles self on his seat.

Tuna told him what brought him and the lady to the palace. At first, the king did not remember whom it was Tuna were talking about until Gayu's name and that of her family was mentioned.

"What!" King Katinu said as he got up from his seat in surprise. "You mean Zizo who has never honored my call went and brought a banished being into my kingdom?" King Katinu added.

He turned to look at the chief priest and, then asked him if he was going to remain mute or say something on the issue at hand. The Chief Priest paid no attention to King Katinu, but went on sniffing around the palace.

"Stop this sniffing around thing and answer the question I just asked you." King Katinu said to the chief priest who still did not say a word to him but kept on doing what he was doing.

His attitude infuriated King Katinu; he gave the chief priest a heavy tap on his back with the stick-like staff in his right hand.

"My king, I am sorry for getting your upset, it is just that something is not right here... something I currently cannot say. My king, the boy that brought the banished one into this kingdom should be summoned right away." Said the chief priest giving a stern look at both Tuna and the lady.

King Katinu called one of his palace guards, then sent him to get him Zizo and the strange lady, then summon every of my council of chiefs. The guard ran out of the palace in a manner that depicts something was after him.

***

Zizo and Gayu were playing hide and seek in the compound when the palace guard came in to deliver the king's message.

"Tell the king we are coming" Zizo said to the palace guard as he turned to continue his hide and seek game.

"Sorry, King Katinu wants both of you now in the palace." The palace guard said placing his hands on his waist.

Zizo and Gayu looked at each other and then followed the guard. The atmosphere at the palace was tensed as King Katinu, chief priest and the council of chiefs sat waiting for Zizo and Gayu. Zizo and Gayu walked into the palace with the palace guard leading the way. Meanwhile, Tuna and the lady that came to report Zizo had gone back to their various destinations.

Zizo greeted everyone that was in attendance and Gayu did same. He politely asked the king the reason why he and Gayu were summoned at the palace.

"Who is this lady that is standing beside you, Zizo?" King Katinu asked Zizo.

Zizo answered him that the lady that was standing beside him was Gayu and that they were a couple. At this, one of the elders stood up and asked Zizo if he did not know that Gayu's family was banished from the land. Zizo gave the chief two answers. He told the chief that he knew her family was banished from the land, and knew that it was her father that was banished, not his entire family. Turning to the king, he told him that from the law of the land, he is fit to marry Gayu. The king was for a second speechless until the chief priest spoke up. He told Zizo that Gayu was a carrier of an evil curse that marrying her was not sanctioned by the gods.

"Did you just say the gods? The same gods that gave her to me? The same gods that protected her when you all left her to die with her family in the woods, wrongly accusing her family and placing curse on her parents. If the gods allowed all that to happen, guess they want to make something beautiful out of that." Zizo said with anger now boldly written all over his face.

"You have two options; send her back to wherever you brought her from, or face the rejection of everyone in this village." King Katinu said getting up from his seat.

Zizo smiled and then answered him that he would rather take the second option and live with the only person that made his life colorful, than associating with people who betray their own. Zizo fired back.

"No matter what, the laws of the land permit us to marry whoever we want to marry so long she is not cursed… so I have found the one I want to marry, let everyone learn how to deal with that." Infuriated Zizo added, not giving Gayu anytime to say a word.

"Well, Zizo has taken the bold step and have chosen his better option. Henceforth, I degree that no one should have a thing to do with either him or this lady that is standing beside him. So shall it be." King Katinu said, lifting up his staff of office.

Zizo thanked him for his judgment; he took Gayu by the hand and then led her out of the palace, smiling as they both walked out of the palace.

"That boy is rude! I wonder what gave him the guts to spoke up in that manner" One of the chiefs whose mouth was opened all along finally spoke.

King Katinu told him he did not care about the thing that gave Zizo the courage to have spoken in that manner; all he knows is that whosoever goes against his decree will be punished accordingly. After saying this to the elders, king Katinu dismissed everyone except the chief priest.

"Do you think he knows about what we did to his parents; how we killed them and then made the villagers believe it was the other community that killed them?" King Katinu asked the chief priest in confusion.

"I do not know what to think anymore... even the awful smell that was in the palace some minutes back have all of a sudden disappeared." The chief priest replied the king, looking more confused than King Katinu.

"Why don't you consult the gods to find out what is behind the smell?" King Katinu asked, looking deep into the chief priest's face.

The chief priest reminded King Katinu that he had not consulted the gods ever since the banishment of Gayu's parents because they were wrongly banished from the land.

"The gods gave me a second chance after we killed the parents of Zizo, but we both misused it when we banished Gayu's parents from the land which later led to their deaths. My king, I strongly believe the gods are up to something, what I am praying for now is that they do not kill us or expose us because the villagers will come after our neck and you know that." The Chief priest said with a shaky voice.

"What was that about" Gayu asked Zizo as they walked into Zizo's house.

"I do not understand what you are saying" Zizo said as he walked to the rear of his house.

"I mean what gave you the effrontery to speak to your king in that manner? Even if you know his secret, you should not have spoken to him in that manner, in front of the top people that hold him in high esteem." Gayu said following Zizo from behind.

Zizo apologized for the way he spoke to him, but told her he did not feel bad talking to him in that manner, that he would do more to anyone that tried to talk him out into ending what he shared with Gayu.

"Do you know what I am thinking Gayu?" Zizo asked, turning to face Gayu.

Gayu wondered what Zizo was thinking, she wondered if he was planning to abscond with her to an unknown place. Her guess was not far from what Zizo was thinking. He pleaded they visit her enchanting word and spend some days there. His words brought joy to Gayu who already was missing her home.

***

The following day, Zizo and Gayu walked the village path holding hands, smiling and chatting without caring about the people that saw them but did not talk to them... some even ran away from them.

"You know I kind of like the way people are seeing us and running away from us, it makes me feel like we are the god they serve." Zizo said still holding Gayu's hands.

"Wondering what kind of god you would be." Gayu said as they walked into the path that led to the enchanting world.

It was night and the stars are shining brightly in Inoko. Everyone was fast asleep allowing the sound of croaking frogs rent the air. Ghoulbraham walked into Tuna's compound, holding a decaying meat that has maggot dripping out from it in his left hand. He took a bite from the meat then vanished into Tuna's room where Tuna was already fast asleep.

"Hey little man!" Ghoulbraham said, giving Tuna a soft tap on his thigh with his right hand.

Tuna woke up but did not see Ghoulbraham, he scented the awful smell that was in the room but still did not see Ghoulbraham.

"I thought we had an agreement never to get yourself involved in what you later got yourself involved in?" Ghoulbraham said revealing himself to Tuna.

"Please who are you and what are you talking about?" Frightened Tuna asked.

"You already know who I am; I do not need further introduction." Ghoulbraham said taking another bite from the decaying meat.

This time, Tuna was already wetting his pant. He begged Ghoubraham not to harm him but Ghoulbraham gave a wicked laugh that told Tuna he was done for.

The sudden disappearance of Tuna was a big shock to everyone in the village, especially Tuna's dad. No one knew what had happened to him, all wondered if he was safe and if he would ever come back again. His father went to the hut of the chief priest to inquiry from the gods if they know Tuna's whereabouts. Like other people that went to the hut of the chief priest seeking for help, the chief priest gave him same answer...he told him that Tuna was safe, that the gods in their kind heart have agreed to go look for him and then bring him back home safe. Though the words are comforting, Tuna's dad left the chief priest's hut feeling he has lost his son and this was true because he never got to see Tuna again for the rest of his life.

7

Zizo was happy with life in the other world as it was a life without worries, fear, and the heat of the sun. It was a perfect world for him.

"When are we going back to the village Zizo?" Gayu asked Zizo who was playing with one of the fireflies in the opened field.

"But we just got here Gayu" Zizo said still playing with the firefly.

"Today makes it the fortnight since we got here, yet you say we just got here?" Gayu said taking a sit beside Zizo.

Zizo was shocked at what she said, to him, it was just some days back they got here, did not know it was already a fortnight.

"Okay, we shall return to Inoko tomorrow but on one condition, and that is if you allow me see the marching back of the fireflies and shining creatures into that thing that looks like moon." Gayu agreed to Zizo's condition.

She promised waking him up the following morning so he would see the fireflies and shining creatures.

Very early the following day while the stars were still shining bright in the sky, Zizo was woken up by Gayu. After the exchanging of greeting, Zizo and Gayu rushed to the environment where the moon-like object was.

"Wow!" Zizo exclaimed as he watched the fireflies and shining creatures return into the moon.

"Yea, I believe their return is more beautiful than their coming out." Gayu said, looking at their return with smile all over her face.

"I agree with you... everything seems to be perfect here. I do not think I will ever get tired of this environment Gayu!" Zizo said as he turns and walks away.

Gayu followed him from behind, and in no distant time, both were back in Inoko village, walking to their house. Nobody saw them because everyone was still asleep. Both rested for some minutes before going to farm to cultivate it. While they worked on the farm, Zizo heard some villagers discussing the sudden disappearance of Tuna and how his father was bedridden because of the news; the villagers were on their way to the palace to ascertain if there was any news on Tuna. Zizo went to meet them to inquire from them what actually happened to Tuna but they ignored him, saying they did not want the wrath of the king and the gods. One of them even said he was sure Tuna's disappearance was because he was Zizo's friend. Zizo could not do a thing about their words but watched them with both hands crossed on his chest as they walked away. The news devastated Zizo as he remembered the good old days spent with Tuna. He could not continue with his farm cultivation but asked Gayu to follow him home. She obeyed without asking him what the problem was. Both walked home in silence.

At home, Zizo cried like a baby, getting some fluids coming out from his nostrils without even paying any attention to it. He grieved in pain as he recalled the good old days spent with Tuna... thought about how they both worked on the farm, went fishing and promises made to each other. Gayu tried talking him out of his pains but she could not. She made him his favorite food but Zizo did not even take a bite from it.

"Please give me some minutes; I want to find out something in the palace." Zizo said as he got up from his seat and then walked out of his compound with tears still coming down his face.

Gayu watched him helplessly and did not know when a tear dropped from her eye.

***

It was afternoon and the scotching sun was up in the sky. However, it did not disturb the people of Inoko as they gathered in the King's compound asking him endless questions on what happened to Tuna and if he would ever be found again. Zizo stood afar of the people that were gathered in the palace. King Katinu told them the story he was told by Tuna's father, how he had woken up and did not see Tuna outside, checked his room but discovered he was not there. He also told them how he had sent out search parties to comb the village for Tuna but still did not get positive report from the search parties.

"Does that mean we are no longer safe in our community?" One of the people spoke up.

"We are safe, and I can assure you that soon, we will get to know what or who exactly is behind the missing of Tuna. However, I will send out another search party today to thoroughly comb the village and bring back Tuna, dead or alive... I hope they be successful this time around!" King Katinu said as he turned and walked into his inner chamber, beckoning on the chief priest to come with him.

Zizo watched in pains as the people walked out of palace in group, muttering words that he could not hear because of his distance from them. Meanwhile, in the inner chamber, King Katinu begged the chief priest to consult the gods on behalf of Tuna, to get answer from the gods that he would tell the people should the new search party he was going to send out return without any positive result.

"My King, I have told you already, I cannot consult the gods. However, I will fortify the searchers so their eyes will be open to any hidden thing when they embark on the search. I assure you that they will return with good result." Said the chief priest in a low tone.

Zizo returned home with a heavy heart and heavy eyes. He thought he would see Gayu at the entrance waiting for him but when he did not, he became scared, and he called out her name as he searched the frontage on the house and the rooms in the house. With his heart panting like that of a person who had just finished running a marathon race, he rushed to the rare of his house where he saw Gayu fast asleep on a chair in front of the tall tree in the compound. He gave a sigh of relieve. He walked up to her and then imagined what would have happened to him if she were not in the compound. After his imagination, Zizo managed to carry Gayu on his back into the room. At night, Zizo narrated what he heard happened to Tuna and how the King had promised to send a search party the following day to look for Tuna.

"Do you think he is still alive Zizo?" Gayu asked as she removed the dishes on the table.

Zizo answered her that every part of him tells him Tuna is dead; however, he hoped he was alive. He too got up and helped Gayu out in clearing the dishes.

Meanwhile, inside strange woods known as forbidden forest by the people of Inoko, on a tall tree in Inoko village, Ghoulbraham feasted on the decomposing body of Tuna while drinking a likely that had awful smell. He enjoyed his meal even though he ate it with a long face. Maybe he was not happy he killed Tuna because he was Zizo's friend or because the death of Tuna had turned the village into a dark town.

"Most humans do not live up to the age that was destined for them because they fail to listen to some important little things they think is not necessary." Ghoulbraham soliloquized after taking a drink from what was in his cup.

He gave a wicked laugh and just when he was about pulling out another body part, there was a loud thunderclap that depicted there was going to be a heavy downpour. And Ghoulbraham was a spirit that never allowed rainwater touch his skin as such, he disappeared.

"Thank the gods it is going to rain tonight, was actually thinking of what to do to the crops on my farm." Zizo said as he lay down in bed.

"The gods are wiser than we are, Zizo; let us always pray we find favor in their eyes." Gayu said as put off the light.

***

The following day, some youths forming up the search party were gathered in front of the palace, to receive some instructions from the king before they would set out. However, the instructions they thought they would receive did not get to them because King Katinu was ill. The chief priest came out and sprinkled some liquids on them, after which he asked them to begin the search. They marched out the palace chanting some warlike songs soon they were combing every nook and cranny of the village. They searched and searched but did not find Tuna until they ventured into the woods, there they saw the remains of Tuna at the feet of a tall tree. Apparently, it had fallen as a result of the heavy downpour of the other night. They were able to identify Tuna through the bracelet that was on his right wrist, a bracelet that was common amongst his family. They plucked some leaves and then wrapped his body in it. Minutes later, the searchers were in the palace carrying Tuna's remains.

Their coming to the palace with Tuna's remains was news with two sides... it made the people happy that they came back successful, but made them sad because they did not bring Tuna back alive, they brought him incomplete. King Katinu managed to come out from his inner chamber wearing a look that showed he was not himself. He applauded the searchers for their success, however asked that the entire village do self-investigation on who actually kidnapped Tuna, killed him and then left his body for some creatures to feast on. He was still speaking when Tuna's dad was rolled on a wheelchair into the palace where upon getting into the compound; saw the mutilated body of his son. They tried hiding the body from him but it was already too late. He could not stand the sight. He held the right side of his chest and then gave up the ghost.

His death threw the entire village into a mourning it never experienced, not because Tuna's dad was a great man, but because he died same day the body of his son was found, and because there was no one to take after all that he had. According to the laws of the land, anyone that dies same day with his or her son or daughter will not be buried but thrown away in the same strange forest where Tuna's body was discovered. That day was a day the entire Inoko inhabitants wished never came.

8

Two years after, everything seemed to be back to normal with the people of Inoko village. There was no case of missing person, seeing strange being in homes and parents dying same day with their kids. Inoko was so peaceful that most of the people forgot Tuna and his family ever lived amongst them, but never forgot the king's decree on Zizo and Gayu. On the other hand, everything seemed to be same in Zizo's house because after many months of being together, they were yet to have a child of their own. This actually made their home pale. Zizo on the other hand tried his best possible to making Gayu happy and live her life with or without baby but she would not understand. One day, he returned from his farm where he had gone to harvest his crops only to find Gayu talking to herself, wishing how she would have loved to have a child, one that she would talk to when Zizo was not around. She wept as she spoke to herself.

"Hi Gayu!" Zizo said taking a sit beside her.

He cleaned the tears on her face and then asked if she would want to spend some time with her with fireflies and shining creatures but she declined. She told him she did not want to see the fireflies, shining creatures or nothing at all, but to see the face of a baby she was yet to conceive.

"I just want to be like every other normal woman in the world!" she said as she let down on her cheeks a stream of tears. "Why don't we see the chief priest for help?" she managed to speak out from her tears.

Zizo told her they could not visit the chief priest because he had never loved them for one day, and because the king's decree was still standing. His answer made Gayu weep more.

"Guess I should spend some time at my place!" Gayu said to Zizo who was by now staring at her with his body still stained in mud.

Zizo requested to go with her to her place but she refused. Her refusal to allow Zizo follow her to the place made him also to turn down her request as he was scared of what would become of her when he was not there... he imagined her committing suicide and so gave a no to her request. He told her to have faith, as they were still very young as such, have a high possibility of having kids of their own. His words though true, somehow found it difficult entering into the heart of Gayu. She insisted on seeing the chief priest for solution and knowing Zizo would again turn down her request, remembered him of his pledge never to turn down her request. At this, Zizo granted her request but told her he would be accompanying her to see the chief priest and this found a way into her heart as she smiled and then asked Zizo to go in and freshen up while she checked the meal she was preparing.

"No!" Gayu cried out from her sleep with sweat all over her body.

Her scream woke Zizo up from his sleep. He clicked on a metal that brings out light and then used it to check the room. When he was satisfied nothing was in the room, he asked Gayu what happened to her.

Gayu told him that she was dreaming, and in her dream, she saw herself carrying a baby that looks kind of strange, "I was cool with the baby even though it looked strange. I was cool with it because I was the one that bore him."

"If you were cool with the baby, why then did you scream out from your sleep?" Zizo asked staring at Gayu's eyes.

Gayu told him that she screamed because the dream she thought was awesome turned out to be a nightmare. She told Zizo that as she was about feeding the baby, the baby coughed and then vomited something that looked like human bone. She told him that while she was busy trying to figure out the baby vomited, maggots started coming out from the bone-like structure that was on the ground, and the baby on her lap turned into a three-eyed creature with big feet, gave her a smile and then disappeared.

"Did you say the baby turned into a three-eyed creature?" Zizo asked with a shaky voice.

"Yes, he was, and with big feet too. Do you know him?" Gayu asked.

Zizo told her he was not sure of what or who the creature was, but that if she should give birth to such a baby, he would be the one to kill him before he wreaks havoc. He held her close until she fell asleep.

The following day while Zizo and Gayu were working on the farm, some inhabitants of the village attacked them with words. They mocked them for not having a child of their own. One of them said Zizo and Gayu where been punished by the gods for their sins. Another advised Zizo to chase Gayu away so he could get himself a better woman that would bear him the one that would keep his lineage going. Zizo reminded them of the decree of King Katinu that forbade them from talking to him and Gayu. He told them he was going to report them to the king and make sure they get punished for violating the king's decree. At this, the people left him and Gayu. However, the damage had already been done as Gayu had long gone home to sob while he was making it out with the people.

Gayu stayed up all afternoon waiting for Zizo to return but he never did. She became worried but did not know where to go look for him. She encouraged herself to start making dinner believing Zizo would return from wherever he was. Without wasting time, she hurried to the kitchen and started making dinner. Zizo's kitchen was one of the finest in Inoko as it was made from fresh bamboo. She did not stay with the food she was preparing like she always did whenever she was cooking, but went patrolling the compound to receive Zizo when he returns. It was dusk, Gayu was long done with the food she was preparing but Zizo was yet to return. In fright, she locked the door and then went out in search for Zizo. Just as she stepped out of the compound, she saw Zizo chatting and laughing with a lady. She called out his name and when Zizo turned and saw her, he left the lady and then ran after Gayu. He met Gayu crying like a baby. He walked up to her but when he tried placing his hand on her shoulder, she pushed his hands away. She accused him of seeing someone else, yet acted like no other person was in the picture except her. She asked him how he managed to be comfortable hurting her and going back on his word. She did not give Zizo any room for explanation as she gave him a resounding slap on his right cheek. Zizo held his cheek, turned to walk away but Gayu pulled him back and then gave him another shocker of his life, she bit him on his shoulder. Zizo was angered by her action; he complimented her action by giving her slaps on her both cheeks, and then asked her to pack out of the house. By now, Gayu was back to her senses, she apologized for her actions but it was already too late as Zizo was hell bent on her leaving the house. In tears, she packed the few things she had at Zizo's place and then cried out of the compound remembering all the good times she spent with him.

"She slapped me for no reason; she did not even give me an opportunity to explain what I was doing with that lady." Zizo said in anger as he walked into his room.

Later that night, Gayu could not sleep in her house, in tears she walked to the field, there she watched the dancing fireflies and wished she could be as happy as they were. While this was going on, Zizo slept peacefully in his house. He saw himself in an all-white environment where the flowers in the environment were white. This environment seemed to be finer than the one where he met Gayu. He went about admiring everything. There was a particular flower that had green petals that caught Zizo's eyes. The flower increased at every step Zizo made toward it. Zizo held a petal in his right hand and admired it. Just as he was about to be taking another petal, there was a flash of lightening that changed the weather, the green flower started turning into Ghoulbraham. The all-white environment turned into a dark environment with scary sounds emitting from it. Zizo turned, made effort to run away but discovered his legs were stuck to the ground. After the flower has fully transformed into Ghoulbraham, Ghoulbraham turned and plucked a straw from a white flower that was beside him. Held the straw in his right hand and it transformed into a whip. Zizo seeing all these things, cried out for help but there was no help as he was all alone in that environment. Ghoulbraham gave a wicked laugh as he walked up to Zizo whose legs were still stuck to the ground. He asked Ghoulbraham confusing questions he was not able to answer. His questions made Zizo wondered if it was Gayu that was speaking through him. He called Ghoulbraham Gayu and then begged him to have mercy on him but the name Gayu made Ghoulbraham gave another wicked laugh, and then with the whip in his right hand, he gave Zizo some painful strokes, not minding where the strokes touched him. Zizo begged for mercy but mercy was far away from him as Ghoulbraham increased the speed with which he was flogging Zizo. Zizo experienced this painful nightmare until it was morning.

As soon as Zizo heard the chipping of the early morning birds, he quickly got himself into his cloth that was hanging on the arm of his bed and then rushed out of the house without even shutting the door. Thank the gods there were no thieves in Inoko if not, that would have been the day when he would have lost all he ever labored for. As soon as he came out of his house, he began a 100-meter race that was never 100 meters but more than 100 meters. He ran and never got tired. His racing velocity made even the rusty leaves on the ground float in the air. When he got to the path that led to Gayu's world, he stopped and questioned himself if he was actually doing the right thing. After some seconds of self-examination, he journeyed down the path and then with a confused facial expression, he jumped into the quicksand. In no distant time, he found himself in the open field that was in Gayu's world. He stood to rehearse what he was going to tell Gayu that would make her forgive him. Just as he was rehearsing, his eyes caught a sight, a glowing sight; it was Gayu sleeping on a fallen tree with fireflies and the shinning creatures hovering around her. He wondered what it meant but enjoyed the sight. He stood transfixed and never noticed that the leaves on which he stood was gradually moving him towards Gayu. And like in a scary movie, he suddenly found himself standing in front of Gayu, and Gayu that was sleeping under the hovering of fireflies and shinning creatures, got up at once and then started questioning him with the fireflies and shinning creatures still hovering around her.

Zizo stammered as he tried explaining things that were not true to Gayu. As if Gayu knew he was telling lies, she reminded him of one of his promises that said he would never lie to her. Upon hearing this, Zizo gave a sigh and then apologized for lies and for asking her to leave his house. He told her he had nothing to do with that lady even though he wanted to start having something to do with her secretly. He went down on his knees and then vowed never to repeat such an act. In tears, Gayu told him she had forgiven him, but begged him to keep to his promises or face the punishments that come on beings that break promises.

"I promise I will not go back on my promise with or without babies of our own." Zizo said while holding Gayu's hands.

"AMEN!" said Ghoulbraham who had long been watching them from a distance.

When Zizo and Gayu turned toward the direction where the amen came from, Ghoulbraham was already gone.

"I think someone is here! Did you come with someone?" Gayu asked Zizo who shook his head, meaning he came alone.

"Well, whatever it is that made that statement will not last another hour in this place." Gayu said, and like she spoke to the fireflies and shinning creatures, they heard and then flew to the direction and other parts of the field.

"They are the guards of this place, nothing is allowed in here unless I okay it, and except the person has my blood flowing in his or her veins." Gayu said now wearing a smile on her face.

Zizo watched her with his mouth wide opened having many thoughts in his mind. Gayu asked him to return to Inoko without her, as she wanted to spend some time with her friendly environment where she could do whatever she wanted to do, and enjoy the company of her friends who are pure in heart and protected her from all aches. Zizo smiled, told her he too would want to enjoy their company as well because it had been long since he last saw them.

"Can you please play me a song from your flute?" Zizo asked staring into Gayu's eyes.

Gayu told him yes but that her flute was in her house at the other side of the field. Taking Zizo by the hand, she pulled him towards the other side of the field.

Days later, Gayu and Zizo returned to Inoko with their hands joined together. They smiled as they walked the part that led to Zizo's house telling each other how they would miss the fireflies and shinning creatures. As they walked, they noticed the worrisome look on the faces of everyone they came across. Initially, both of them thought it had something to do with the decree made because of them as after the decree, no inhabitant of Inoko ever smiled at them. Their attitude also gave Gayu some thoughts the day she saw Zizo smiling while talking to a lady the other night.

"I think something is not right." Zizo said, disrupting their chat on fireflies and shining creatures. Gayu sighed, just as she was about replying Zizo, two inhabitants of the village walked toward them discussing of a certain lady from the other village that was found dead with some of her body parts missing.

From their description, Zizo knew the lady they spoke about was the same lady he was with the night he did not return home. He removed his hands from Gayu's and then crossed them on his chest like someone that is suffering from cold. He watched the two people as they walked pass them still chatting about the lady and what her death might cause the village.

"Do you know the lady they are talking about?" Gayu who has been watching Zizo's countenance asked.

Zizo told her that he rarely knew the lady but that the lady was the one he was standing with the night he did not return home.

"Pardon me, but that lady should not have been killed!! She was just an orphan that strayed away from her village because she was searching for a greener pasture." Zizo said with tears almost dripping down his cheeks.

Gayu consoled him, told him that the gods are wise. Trying to cheer Zizo up, she told him that what he should be bothering himself on someone that was already dead, but bothered himself on the possibility of war from the other village. Like her plan worked perfectly well on Zizo, Zizo turned at her, gave her a smile and then told her that should there be any war from the other village, he would just pack some of his properties and then escaped to Gayu's environment. He told Gayu that he even preferred staying in the other environment than Inoko. Both laughed as they journeyed home, no longer minding the frowning faces of the other people they met on their way home.

The palace was filled with community chiefs chatting on the death of the lady that was from the other village. They were so engrossed in the topic of their discussion that they did not even noticed when King Katinu and the chief priest walked in. King Katinu took his sit and then cleared his throat. His act brought the chiefs back to their senses. He cleared his throat again and then spoke up. He told the people that he had been inside discussing with the chief priest on what the gods had to say about the occurrence. Upon hearing this, the chiefs all directed their looks to the chief priest and then back again to the king. The king told them that the gods had advised they send emissaries to the other village explaining to them that they were not the ones that killed the lady.

"Sorry my lord, do you think the other village king will believe what you just said, knowing they are our arch enemy?" one of the chiefs asked King Katinu.

Sensing King Katinu had no answer to the question, the chief priest told them that the gods had agreed to go with the emissaries and that they would come back with good news. Like the chief priest communicated with the gods, the emissaries went and returned from the other village without any issue from the village, even though the mutilated body of the lady could cause a stir, they accepted the corpse and allowed sleeping dogs lie with a warning never to again receive such news from Inoko. When the emissaries returned and broke the news from the other community, King Katinu and his chief priest were praised for using their wisdom to avert a war that would have claimed lives from both sides. At this, King Katinu threw a party for everyone in the village except Zizo and Gayu who were still under the decree.

***

It was evening but the moon was yet to take its position in the sky. The birds were retiring to their nests and the trees were beginning to have their last dance for the day. The chief priest was outside his hut, making some lineage prayers to his ancestors, thanking them for pleading to the gods on his behalf, thus making the village peaceful for everyone in the village. He was still in the mood of thanksgiving when Zizo and Gayu walked into his compound. He paid no attention to them but went on with his thanks. Zizo and Gayu called his name but he ignored them, when he had finished giving thanks, he asked them angrily what gave them the guts to enter his place that they should leave before he strikes them to death, Gayu and Zizo pleaded with him and asked him for help, but before they could finish their sentence he shouted at them and told them to get out that he will not help them, that he doesn't help forbidden people, then Zizo told him that there was a time when the chief priest was young and needed help that his father helped him and that the chief priest swore to help anyone from his father's linage, then the chief priest laughed and told him that he didn't mean what he said then and chased them away from his shrine, then they left.

On their way back they saw a strange old woman carrying woods on her head and walking helplessly. The woman begged them to help her carry the woods, it sounded somehow but because Zizo was a kind person he decided to help the woman to carry the woods to the woman's house. As they were going to the woman's house, the old woman asked Zizo if she can ask him some questions and he said yes then the woman asked him to tell her about himself, then he told her about himself and his father, and then she asked him about Gayu then he told her who Gayu was. The old woman smiled and said that they would make a very good couple. When they got to her house, Zizo took the woods to the rear of her house and he dropped it there and came out. Before he left the woman thanked him and told him that because he is a kind and humble fellow, he should tell her what he wants in his marriage. Zizo thought for a moment and then he turned his attention to Gayu and both smiled at each other. Then he turned his attention to the old woman and told her that they are in search for a child, that they have been looking for a child over the last two years and they could not get any. He spoke that they have been going to different people for help but no one wants to help them because the community people were told not to speak to them nor help them.

The old woman then told them that they would have a child but on one condition, the couple rejoiced and asked what was the condition? The aged woman then told that for them to have a child they have to sleep under the forbidden tree known as Bukinato for three days and when Gayu wants to deliver the child, it must be under the same tree or else she will die while delivering the child elsewhere. For a moment, the joy of the couple seized but still Gayu and Zizo thanked the old woman and returned to their house.

The next day they went to the tree known as Bukinatu, there they slept for three days, the third day Gayu became pregnant, both of them were happy and rejoiced, they also thanked the gods for giving them a child unknowing to them that the child was a god, there they slept. On the fourth day they went back to their house, as they were going to their house, they came across a witch in the community. On seeing them, the witch sensed that Gayu was pregnant, due to the fact that she already knew that they were going to give birth to a god whom he still did not know what god they were going to have. She exclaimed, and after that she shook her head and walked away, in her mind she told herself that she had to do something to stop the pregnancy before Gayu would deliver, while on the other hand Gayu and Zizo were staring at her as she was going and also were asking themselves why did the witch shake her head, but because no one usually spoke to them they decided to mind their business and went home straight. When they got home, they relaxed themselves and made some jokes about the name they were going to give to their child; if it was a male or female, while on the other side when the witch got to her temple she sat down and started thinking on ways to eliminate the pregnancy, then a thought entered her mind to kill the Gayu in her dream.

When it was night and everyone was asleep Gayu had a dream and in the dream she saw herself tied on a tree, then she saw the witch coming towards her direction with dagger on her hands and she couldn't do anything about it, when she got there she stabbed her in her stomach with the dagger but the stomach didn't tear, she did it again but the same thing happened, suddenly she found out that she could not raise the hand that she used to stab the stomach of Gayu, then she saw blood coming out the eyes of Gayu, immediately the stomach of Gayu opened and the child in her womb came out from the womb, the child made the witch to kneel down, then he pointed his hands towards the witch and immediately the body of the witch started dividing and then she fell into pieces. Then Gayu jumped up from the bed terrified. This woke Zizo up from his sleep and asked his wife what the problem was, so she told him everything but Zizo consoled her and they both slept. The next morning there was information that the witch is dead. When the news got to them, Gayu remembered the dream she had and she looked at her womb and smiled. The whole village was silent for a week and after a week the community went back to normal, but as each day breaks, the pregnancy continued to eat the inner body of Gayu and this made her weak, Zizo did all he could but the situation didn't change.

9

It was a sunny day as usual in Inoko and her inhabitants went about their duties. Children were seen playing with sands in their various homes with their mothers tending to home chores; some men were at their farms working while some were at home lazing about in the name of looking after the home, protecting it from invaders that never existed. Zizo was among the men that did not go to farm; however, he was not lazing about but was not feeling too well because he had not sleep for some days, always keeping watch on Gayu who was in deep pain as a result of the baby that was in her womb. A baby that grew in the womb faster than every normal baby, not because Gayu was properly taken care of by Zizo, which was true, but because the baby was also feeding on Gayu's blood and her internal organs. Zizo came out of the room carrying a bowl that had a colored liquid in it. It was actually prepared from the things given to them by the aged woman. He walked up to Gayu who was lying on the leave bed that was specially prepared by Zizo because of her condition. He walked up to her and had her sit up so he could administer the liquid substance to her. Gayu looked at him, though in pains, managed to give him a smile.

"Thanks for keeping to all the promises you made to me the day we embarked on this journey. I wish to see many happy days with you Zizo." Gayu said as she received the bowl from Zizo who was also smiling at Gayu.

Just as Gayu was about taking it, she went into labor and the weather suddenly became cloudy. There was a heavy wind but then it was neither raising dust, nor destroying things. At first, Zizo did not understand what was happening to Gayu until she gave him a hard knock on his head. He did not even hear Gayu's request because he was busy wondering about what kind of wind was blowing. When Zizo was fully back to his senses, Gayu in labor pain requested he took her to the tree, which the old woman had told them to be at whenever she was in labor. Zizo ran into the room to get some items that were usually used on pregnant women of Inoko. When he came out, Gayu was no more on the leafy bed but on her way out of the compound, staggering as she walked. He rushed to her, allowed her rest a part of her on his shoulder.

"I may not know the extent of the aches you are currently experiencing, what I know is that you will pull throw it, I mean, we will pull through it." Zizo said with a smile as he helped her out of the compound.

Everyone in the village wondered what strange wind was blowing. Those that were outside playing rushed into their houses, even those that were working on their farms ran to their various homes. None wanted to be caught outside his home because they feared the safety of their families.

While they journeyed out of the compound with the weather now getting darker by the minutes, they met the lady that wished Zizo married her running with a farming implement that looked like a basket. Zizo begged she assisted him in carrying Gayu to the tree, which the aged woman told them about. Sadly, all Zizo's pleas were ignored as the lady instead of assisting Zizo and Gayu, made mockery of them with ill words, she even went as far as telling them she was among the people that never wished Gayu became pregnant. She violated the king's order, which said that nobody should talk to both Zizo and Gayu but did not care because she saw that as her only avenue of getting her own pound of flesh back from Zizo.

"Well, as both of you go to only where the gods know, I say you do not have the chance to come out of it alive... that is my wish or should I say my blessing to you two." The lady said as she gave a scornful laugh and then walked away.

Zizo was vexed at her but could not go after her because of the aches Gayu was having. Like an exhausted man who just finished fighting a battle, Zizo staggered on with Gayu as she groaned in aches. It was a journey Zizo wished they never embarked upon. Zizo and Gayu defiled the weather as they journeyed on. Few meters to the forbidden tree, Gayu was already exhausted, she had no strength again left in her, and her baby was almost out of her body. She groaned in aches, telling Zizo she could no longer journey on to the forbidden tree. Zizo encouraged her to try as they were already closed to the tree. She tried again but could not. At this, Zizo decided to have her on his back. He bent his back and then asked her to climb on him. Zizo made attempt to carry her but failed as her budging stomach did not allow her. He placed his hands under her in an attempt to carry her in his hands, but she was too heavy for him to carry. He tried again but this time; Gayu fell on the ground and could not stand up again. She was already having her baby there. While she screamed in labor pains, Zizo prayed the words of the aged woman did not come to pass in Gayu's life. He quickly gathered some fresh leaves and then made a bed for Gayu to lie on and have her baby. Gayu rolled herself on top of the leaves. At every push she made, the lightning and thunder responded to it, finally when the baby came, the baby was a male; it had a green skin and had three eyes with two big feet. Though the baby was strange yet Zizo was happy, never recalled the dreams of a three-eyed greenish creature that tormented him whenever he was alone or had an issue with

Zizo. Zizo held the baby in his arms with joy and then showed it to Gayu, without noticing she was bleeding profusely. Gayu touched the baby and smiled at the baby, hiding what she was going through from Zizo.

"What do you suggest we call him Zibo?" Gayu asked still wearing a smile on her face as she admires the baby.

"I really do not know; wait let me take a closer look at him." Zizo said as he moved closer to the baby for admiration.

Like the baby knew Zizo was going to admire him, he gave Zizo a smile that revealed his perfect set of it.

"What! Did you see that Gayu?" Zizo asked Gayu in fright.

Gayu told him she did not see anything other than a cute green baby in her arms. She was still on her explanation when Zizo remembered all his past dreams and how he had promised Tuna he would kill the baby should he happen to give birth to him. Zizo moved slowly away from Gayu with different thoughts of what he was going to do to the baby.

"Why are you moving away from us Zizo? Is everything alright?" confused Gayu asked Zizo as he moved away.

Zizo told her there was nothing wrong with him. He told her he was just taking some few steps backward so he could get a better view of the baby. At this, Gayu gave a faint smile and then asked him what they would name the baby. But, still, no answer came from Zizo. Now, Zizo was already using his eyes to survey the area to see if there was any hard object or sharp object with which he would kill the baby. By now, the rain was already pouring down heavily, making it more difficult for Zizo to notice Gayu's blood.

"Our baby looks like the tale my parents once told me when I was still very young. They told me that the creature was..." Gayu was still talking when Zizo cut in.

He told her that the creature her parents told her about is the same creature they have given birth to and if they did not take proper care of him now by killing it, it would grow up and destroy everything and everyone he ever set his eyes upon, especially those that upset him or had upset the gods of the land.

"Gayu, give me the baby and let us get rid of it now that we still can." Zizo said with his arms stretched out, ready to receive Ghoulbraham from Gayu's arms.

Just then, Zizo found out that she was bleeding seriously. He gathered other leaves with which he tried stopping the bleeding but could not as it was already too late. Gayu had already lost much blood that she could no longer talk properly. Zizo did all he could to make her talk but the more he tried, the less he achieved. He noticed Gayu was passing away. With the little strength left in her, she begged Zizo to name the child and then promised never to allow any harm come close to him. in tears, Zizo promised her that he would not kill the baby no matter what happened, he placed his right hand on his chest and then vowed not to allow any harm come near the baby as long he still had breath in his nostrils. at this, Gayu gave another faint smile that revealed the dimples on her face. He took a deep look at the baby and just as he was about giving the baby a name, he discovered Gayu was no longer breathing and the baby in her arms was beginning to fall down. He grabbed the baby before he would touch the ground, placed the baby on the leafy bed. He knelt beside Gayu's corpse, shook her to wake up but she never did. He held her in his arms, called her name many times, but she never responded as she was already far away from the world. In pains, Zizo promised not to kill the baby that he would raise the child no matter what happened, and then gave a laugh that made it look like he had gone mad.

"Thank goodness I never gave you a name, would have unknowingly called you a name that would send you back and then failed in my promises made to Gayu. As long as I live, you will become what you want to become and execute everything you want to execute.

Inoko needs a great turn around." Zizo said still broken at heart as he lifted the baby up to the sky and allowed the rain-wash him.

He watched as the heavy rain washed away Ghoulbraham's umbilical cord. Zizo put the baby on his back as he wrapped Gayu's corpse in the leafy bed and then carried it on his shoulder into the village. The inhabitants of Inoko watched him from their windows as he journeyed under the heavy rain carrying the corpse of Gayu on his head and Ghoulbraham on his back. None came out to ask what he had on his head or ask him to leave the rain and get a shelter for himself and the baby he was carrying on his back. None took pity on him; they all watched and shook their heads not in pity for what he was going through, but for his stupidity for not working with the king's order. Zizo cried and wished he never came from that village. His tears were so much that one could see them in the rain. He struggled in aches as struggled down the sleepy path that led to his house. When he got home, he dropped Gayu's corpse inside the room and then the baby on his favorite chair, the one he always allowed Zizo sit on. He went out in the heavy rain to the place where he usually kept his farming implements. From there he took out his shovel and then headed for the tree behind his house.

"You are my joy, you brought joy into my life... here is the spot I cherished most, the spot you once shared with me. I do not know if you would like it but I think laying you down here will gladden your spirit. I wish you never have to leave me this soon!" Broken Zizo said as he dug up a grave for Gayu.

In no time, he was done with the grave. He went inside, gently carried Gayu's corpse and then buried in front of the tree, the spot he dug for her. He took a sit on the ground beside the grave, staring at the grave while it still rained heavily. Zizo's grief made him forgot there was a newly born baby inside his room that needed his attention. He stayed all day under the rain staring at the grave and remembering the times he spent with Gayu until it was late in the evening. In fact, it was the last thought about Gayu asking him to promise never to allow any harm come near their baby that brought him back to the reality of having a child who was all alone in the room and needed to be taking care of. He stood up in pain and then walked to the frontage of the house. He walked into the room but did not see the baby in the room. All he saw was a scattered room, the bed was turned upside down, chairs and some other things too. He became scared and wondered what would have happened to his baby. He wondered how the baby would survive the night alone in this cruel village. Some other thoughts like how would the spirit of Gayu take his failure to keep to a promise that was made on the same day and what if the baby was killed, would not it come and avenge his death starting from him?

He was still in deep thoughts when he heard the sound of rustling leaves at the side of his house. Without having a second thought and with a blood-stained eye, he rushed to where his farming implements were, took out a sharp knife and then rushed towards the side of his house. As he rushed, he heard the sound of a baby cackling. This made him hasten his steps. When he got there, He saw the baby standing on his feet, not staggering as he played with the rustling leaves under the rain. For a second, he thought he was dreaming until the baby ran up to him and then gave him a tight hug on his ankles because he was still young even though he had teeth in his mouth and could stand on his legs, his height was still that of a newly born baby. Zizo tried looking down on the baby with the intention of playing with his curly hair, but caught the baby smiling at him. Yes, it was a smile, a cheerful one from the baby, but from the look that was on his face, it looked as if the baby was giving a wicked smile.

"I will protect you no matter who you are or what you look like, or what the people think about you." Zizo said with a little grin on his face as he now played with the baby's curly hair.

He might have heard a lot about Ghoulbraham, but have never experienced one. More so, never heard they could have a perfect set of teeth and stand on their feet on the first day of their birth. He carried the baby up in his arms and then took him inside.

"Please wait here while I go prepare something for us to eat." Zizo said to the baby as he placed him on one of the chairs that was still standing on its fours.

Now having the responsibilities of being a father, Zizo made sure he removed every sharp object and everything that might cause the baby harm. As if the baby heard him and was hungry, he cooed and then gave Zizo a smile that made him think there were approval signs from the baby. He left the baby and then using some leaves, he made an umbrella for himself before going to the kitchen to make what him and the baby would eat. Zizo often ran from the kitchen to the room where the baby was to check on him, but on every return to where the baby was, he met the room scattered. However, he did not get angry or yelled at the baby. He instead gave the baby a smile a smile and then hurriedly re-arrange the room before dashing out to the kitchen. He gave a sigh of relieve when the meal was ready. He got a bowl and then dished his food and that of the baby into it, this he brought to the room where the baby was still wearing a smiling face, and rearranging the messy room. he sat on the bed with the baby on his laps and the bowl of food on one of the chairs.

"Baby, dinner is ready, it is crunchy. I made it specially for you because I know you will like it. do not mind your dad's meal, I know it might not taste sweet in your mouth but you just have to start learning how eat it because it what both of us will be eating... I do not plan having a second wife, giving you a second mother." Broken but smiling Zizo said to the baby.

Again, it was as if the baby heard him, he gave Zizo another smile. At this, Zizo sighed; he dipped a spoon into the bowl and then tried feeding the baby with it. When the baby saw the spoon coming towards his, he grabbed Zizo's hands and then used it to feed himself. When the spoon got into his mouth, he smiled, but when Zizo was about complimenting the baby' smile, the baby spat out what was in his mouth. This got Zizo confused. He told the baby sorry and then used the back of his right palm to check the temperature of the food in the bowl.

"Oh! I am so sorry! I did not realize it was hot. Okay, I will fan it and after I am sure it is warm, I shall feed you." Zizo said, feeling sorry for hurting the baby.

He dropped the baby on the bed, plucked out a leaf from his leafy bed and then used it to fan the food. Like he said, when the food was warm, he tried feeding the baby but again the baby spat out the meal. This got Zizo more confused. He attempted to feed the baby but all his attempts failed. He played with the baby thinking that when the baby was very hungry, he would not have to reject or spit out his meal. But this plan too failed as the baby not only rejected the meal, he kicked the bowl and made it fall facing the ground. Zizo got upset at this but when he was about to be spanking the baby, he gave Zizo a smile that made Zizo looked with pity upon him.

"Oh!" Zizo hit his forehead. "I am the one to be blamed for this!" Pointing at the bowl on the floor. "I made you a crunchy meal, thinking because you have teeth you will like it, not knowing that these features do not change the fact that you are still a newly born baby and milk is what you need, not chewable meals. Please hold on while I get you milk to drink." Zizo said now staring at the baby with smile all over his face.

He dashed out of the room and in no time, returned carrying a glass of milk in his hand. with smile on his he again carried the baby on his laps and then tried feeding him with the milk. But again, the baby spat out the milk, wearing a frown on his face. At this time, Zizo was completely out of ideas on to get the baby. He was still in deep thoughts when the baby started crying at the top of his voice.

His voice was so loud that it shook the four corners of the room. It was so loud that Zizo could no longer hear the sound of the heavy rainfall that was dropping on the roof of his house.

"Being a father is not easy, would have been easy if only you were here Gayu!" Zizo said staring at Gayu's picture frame with tears coming down his eyes.

He cried as he rubbed the curly hair on the baby's head. The baby stooped crying, he cooed and soon fell asleep on Zizo's laps. He carefully placed the baby on the bed, took a deep breath and then lay beside the baby, staring into the empty air remembering the good times spent with Gayu.

***

The following day, Zizo woke up to find himself alone in the bed, he jumped up in panic but saw the baby sitting on the floor eating the crunchy food that was on the floor, the same food he rejected the previous night. By now, the food was already bad and had an awful smell.

"Hey! Do not eat that!" Zizo said as he jumped down from the bed.

He rushed up to the baby and then collected the bowl from him.

"This food is bad; it is not good for your health! You are hungry right?" Zizo asked the baby expecting to get a smile for a yes or a frown for a no from the baby, but he did not get any of these from the baby.

He carried him up, looked into his face and then asked him the same question. Instead of the options he had in his mind, he got the shocker of his life; the baby spoke. For a second he thought he imagined the sound that came out of the baby's mouth until the baby spoke again, telling him that he was hungry and would not want to eat any food other than the spoilt food that was on the floor.

"You just spoke?" Frightened Zizo asked the baby still in his arms.

"Yes, I did papa, I am hungry and need something in my stomach." The baby said as he tried bringing himself down from Zizo's arms.

"But eating bad meal will make you ill!" Zizo said trying to make the baby see reasons why he should not eat the meal.

"To you it is not good eating this kind of meal, but to me, it is just what I need to survive."

At this, Zizo wondered in his heart if the baby he was carrying was not the monster he had being hearing of. He carefully dropped the baby down and watched him devour the bad meal from where he was standing.

"Enjoy your meal while I go make the compound neat." He said as he walked out of the house, leaving the baby to enjoy his meal.

When he came out of his room, he saw debris everywhere in his house. he paid no attention to the debris and did not even think of how to get them out of his house. He walked slowly to the where he kept one of his leafy chairs, took it and then sat under the tree facing Gayu's grave. Nobody saw him but if they had, it would have seemed to them Zizo was thinking about Gayu and missing her. However, Gayu was not even, what was in him mind. On the other hand, maybe she was; she was the last thing he had in his mind. What was in Zizo's mind was what it was he had given birth to? There was confusion in his mind. He did not know if it was Ghoulbraham she had given birth to or another creature he knew nothing about. The thought of how to find out about the real identity of the baby and how to live with him were in his mind. And the only person he could think of that that had answers to his question was the aged woman that prophesied about the baby.

"Should I see the woman with Gh... what am I trying to do? Calling his name and then make him disappear to only the gods know where? No, I will not all his name; I will go with him to look for the aged woman." Zizo said with an expression that showed that he was confused.

He looked at the grave and wished Gayu was alive to share this.

"But why did Gayu make me promise not to do away with this baby that..." Zizo was still on his words when the baby ran up to him calling him papa with outstretched hands.

He smiled and every of his past thoughts except for the thought of meeting the aged woman left his mind.

"Papa, you look terrible, I think you should get yourself food, the worms in your stomach are not doing your face any good." The baby said as he stared into Zizo's eyes and then jogged around his mother's grave, his curly hair falling off of his head.

Zizo watched in awe wondering how a newly born baby could be that brilliant.

10

It was still morning and there was panic in the entire village of Inoko as everyone woke up to see their compounds not in the same way they saw it before running into their rooms for safety during the heavy downpour. The ones that left their homes for farm works in the hands of their partners to take care could not do anything on the farm as their crops had been uprooted by the wind. As if the gods were angry with them, the flood swept away all the uprooted crops, leaving nothing for them to take home. the king woke up and discovered that his palace had been dealt with by the heavy rain. He thought it was just his palace only until the inhabitants of Inoko started trooping into his palace, some wailing and others murmuring. Their grieve was so much that they paid no attention to his call asking them to be quiet and let one of them tell him why the sudden visit at his palace when there was no call for it. He turned and called on one of his palace guards whom he sent to go quickly to the chief priest's house and get him to the palace.

Even though the people heard King Katinu sending the guards to fetch the chief priest, they acted like they did not as they kept murmuring, making it impossible for all to hear what the other was saying. They could only hear what the person standing in front of them was saying. The sun was shining brightly in the sky but its heat could not dry up the flood that was in the chief priest's compound, as he too was not left out from the disaster, as one side of the blocks in his house had fallen down. As a matter of fact, Zizo's compound seemed to be the only compound that was not really damaged. When he got there, he saw the chief priest checking on the dead animals that littered his compound. The sight was not a good one as not a single animal in his compound was alive. The chief priest wondered why the rain did not destroy Zizo's compound, Zizo then greeted the chief priest and they exchanged greetings, just after exchanging greetings, the guard of king Kitanu came and told the chief priest that the king seeks his presence in the palace.

"I hope all is alright with the king?" The chief priest asked still staring at the dead animals that lay about in his compound.

"How can the king be alright when everyone in the village is in his compound screaming and asking him questions about the heavy storm of yesterday, they are making the compound unbearable for him." Said one of the palace guards that was sent.

The other servant added that the king has sent them to call the chief priest because he believed he was the one that had answers to their questions. Upon hearing this, the chief priest sighed and then walked into his hut, leaving the guards to themselves. Minutes later, he walked out of his hut holding his staff in his right hand and a bag on his left shoulder. He allowed the palace guards to lead the way as he walked behind them chatting some words that were known only to him. In no distant time, the chief priest and the palace guards walked into the palace and the people rejoiced feeling that the solution to their questions has arrived. The guards made way for the chief priest to pass through to where the king was standing as the crowd that was in the palace was doubled the number that was there before they went to call the chief priest. Soon, there was calmness in the palace as the chief priest threw on the ground some items that were in his bag. Everyone, including King Katinu watch the chief priest with expectations written on their faces.

The chief priest said some things to the items on the ground, picked them up and then threw them again on the floor. After some seconds, the chief priest lifted up his head and then spoke to the hearing of everyone. He told them that the storm of the previous night did not just happen but that a great evil has been done in the communicated and if not taken care of on time, will lead to the extinction of the village. At this, everyone including the king became scared, he turned his head to look at King Katinu and when he saw that the king looked at him, he shook his head in a way that sent a scary message of to the king.

"I believe you all heard what the chief priest said? I also want to believe that some of you here will have an idea of what he is talking about. Not going to impose or sanction anyone, but ask you tell me who it is that is behind our misfortune and threatens our extinction." King Katinu said in a type of voice he never used while addressing his people.

Everyone stared at each other, asked one another to know if any has answer that would put an end to their impending nightmare.

***

"Are you sure these are all the people in our community my king?" The chief priest asked the king after seeing that no answer was coming from the people that were gathered in the palace.

"How would I know when they all came here on their own accord?" King Katinu said, using his eyes to scan through the people that were present at his palace. "I think every family is here except the Braham's family." King Katinu said after being sure about the people that were there at the palace.

"You mean Zizo's family?" The chief priest asked. "They are not ought to be here my king, they..." the chief priest was still talking when one of the inhabitants at the palace said she believed it was Zizo that caused the heavy downpour and the impending doom.

At this, everyone, including the chief priest and King Katinu turned to look at her.

"What did you just say?" King Katinu asked the lady who spoke.

"I said I believe Zizo is the one that is responsible for the heavy downpour of yesterday. I said that because while there was heavy wind and the rain was falling down seriously, I saw Zizo carrying something that had the length of one of us on his head, this was wrapped in leaves so I could not see who it was he carried on his head. And on his back was a creature that has green color and big feet. The creature looked like a newly born. And as they walked, Zizo cried like someone that desecrated the land, seeking the face of the gods but did not get mercy for his sins." The lady concluded.

"Ho!" Everyone exclaimed and then started murmuring amongst themselves.

The murmuring was not loud and this made it impossible for the king and the chief priest to hear what they were saying. King Katinu silenced them with an angry voice and then ordered them to speak up or face his wrath.

The eldest person in their midst walked out; "My king, long may you live. We were saying same thing because majority of us here are witnesses to what this lady said, pointing at the lady said. We saw Zizo carrying that unknown thing on his head and a strange looking creature on his back. As a matter of fact, some of the youths here saw him when he was burying whatever it was, he was carrying and playing with the green creature and my king. Without doubt, we know there is more to Zizo than we know."

The man was still talking when King Katinu screamed and then ordered his guards to go and fetch him Zizo, never to return without him.

"Let us start from there" The king said as he walked to his leafy throne to have his seat.

***

"You are cute and unique, never have I seen your kind." Zizo said to Ghoul who was on his bag as they walked down the path that led to the aged woman's hut.

"Where are we going to papa?" The baby asked stretching his head in an attempt to see Zizo's face.

Zizo told him they were going to see and old friend of his and his mother, a friend he believed the baby would know. At the mention of mother, the baby asked Zizo the whereabout of his mother. Zizo sighed and with a shaky voice, told the baby about Gayu and how she died while giving birth to him.

"Sorry papa, sorry mama died. I never planned what happened to her." The baby said as he now placed his head on Zizo's back. "but papa, is that the reason why we are walking all alone on this pathway?" The baby asked again now removing his head from Zizo's back.

Zizo told him the mother was not the reason why they were on the path, that he needed to verify some things he would like to keep to himself. The baby cooed.

"You want to know more about me, right?" Zizo froze upon hearing this from the baby because he just spoke what he had in his mind.

He was going to the aged woman's place to find out from her if the baby was Ghoul or some other creature. He never spoke to the baby or answer any of his questions until they got to the aged woman's hut.

"Greetings to you" Zizo said as he stood in front of the hut looking at the aged woman who was inside the hut smoking, waiting for her to ask him to come in. The aged woman who by now is having difficulty in seeing, raised her head up and after some seconds recognized Zizo and then asked him to come in.

"I can see that your prayers have been answered by the good gods of your land! What brought you here and where is the lady you were always with?" The aged woman asked as she settles herself back into the chair she was sitting on when Zizo came in, still holding her tobacco pipe in her right hand.

"She is no more." Zizo said with tears now flowing freely on his cheeks.

"What! You both did not do what I asked you to do?" She said stretching her head forward to have a closer look at Zizo who was still standing with the baby on his back.

"Take your seat and tell me all that happened and why you are here." She said as she went back to her former sitting position.

Zizo brought down the baby from his back, took a sit opposite the aged woman and then placed his baby on his thighs.

"Gayu took in just as you predicted. I gave her everything her body needed to stay healthy but got the opposite. She kept becoming skinny by the day despite all she ate, and kept complaining of weakness, like she was experiencing shortage of blood. And some days back while we were catching fun, she went into labor and before we could get to the tree, she gave birth to our baby, the baby I am holding. And then gave up due to excess bleeding. Maybe she would have been alive if it did not rain that day; the heavy rain made it impossible for me to see what was happening to her." Zizo said wiping the tears on his cheeks with the back of his left hand. the baby on the other hand nodded his head to everything he saw in the room.

It was as if he had been to the room before that day.

"Sorry for your loss Zizo the aged woman said sympathetically after taking a deep draw from her tobacco pipe, well, what happened to Gayu was part of her destiny. She was made for that purpose. She sacrificed her life for the life you are holding on your thighs because it takes a life to bring a life. Even if she had managed to get to the tree, she still would have died. Zizo, some things are not for us to understand, but for us to live with." The aged woman said as she tried dangling herself on the chair, she was sitting in.

Zizo watched the woman in surprise. "Well, I am here to find out some things about this…"

"About the baby you are carrying?" The aged woman cut in while Zizo was yet to finish his statement.

She asked Zizo to hand over the baby to her and he did. When she received the baby, she admired him, after some seconds, put the baby down, and then bowed to him in a manner that made Zizo open his mouth and wonder what she was doing.

"I am so blessed to have witnessed your coming great one, as long as I live, I will see to it that you accomplished your mission, master." The aged woman said still bowing her head with the baby placing his hand on the woman's head as if he was blessing her or saying amen to all she said.

While this was going on and Zizo's mouth still wide opened, a fly that was enjoying itself buzzing the room mistakenly flew into Zizo's mouth and he swallowed it before he could do a thing about it. He coughed and when he regained himself, asked the baby to come to him and he obeyed like the little child that he was. Zizo carried him and placed him on his thighs as the aged woman returned to her sitting position.

"You see Zizo, the baby you are carrying is the bringer of death on everyone that had sinned against the gods, everyone that will sin against the gods and everyone that will want to pose as obstruction to his mission. You wonder why your baby has a perfect set of teeth, why he could walk even when he is just a day old, and I guess he has started talking as well? You wonder why he grows every second. You wonder why he has three eyes. You wonder why he does not have hair on his head. You wonder if he is the one you once heard about or another creature you know nothing about. He is still the same creature. He could do these things and more he is yet to do because in him lies the powers of his mother and his. He possessed with different powers so do not get upset or go crazy when he does unusual things." While the aged woman was still talking, the baby would stare at Zizo's face and then give a loud laugh in affirmation to what she was saying.

"Do not ever make him angry for he is an unforgiving god, do not false him into doing or receiving what he does not want because it will bring down his wraths on you. Be a good father and you will appreciate the gods for blessing you with one of them." The aged woman concluded with a low smile that revealed the only tooth that was in her mouth.

"I shall do just as you advised and hope I live to see the fulfillment of the great prophesy." Zizo said as he stood to take his leave, carrying the baby in his hands.

Just as he was about walking out of the room, the aged woman told him to never to feed the baby with fresh meals but decaying meals and never try to rearrange whatever the baby scattered because the baby likes staying in a messy environment.

"He is a disaster god and lives in places that do not look good." The aged woman added.

"Wow! I am in for the adventure of a lifetime! Is there any other thing you will like to let me know?" Zizo asked the woman now trying to wear a smiling face.

The aged woman smiled, she told him there are but she would gradually unfold them. She bid them farewell as she watched them walk down the path that led to their village.

"Son, you are indeed a package not to be played with, but handle with care. I am sorry for not answering the numberless questions you asked about your mother while we were going to see that your disciple." At the hearing of disciple, the baby gave a smile.

"Well papa, I know I have met her before but cannot currently tell where or how. Back there, she said so many things I really do not know, and when I placed a hand on her head, I was trying to feel the texture of her hair." The baby said looking at Zizo's face because Zizo was carrying him on his chest.

"Well, I really do not want to go into that, just want to answer the question you asked on where I met your mom." Zizo told the baby, not paying attention to the emptiness of the village.

"Oh! So, tell me where you met my mama." The baby asked with enthusiasm.

Zizo told him he is not going to tell him but to take him to the place. This made the baby leap in excitement on Zizo's chest as they journeyed on.

***

The palace guards arrived Zizo's house, called out but did not get any reply. They called again and when they did not get any reply, they searched the compound as the rooms were all locked from the outside and so could not go into them. they waited for Zizo to return but he never did. They stayed until the sun started setting but still Zizo did not return. They could not report to the palace because King Katinu ordered them not to return without Zizo. They were there until another set of guards came to call them to the palace. It was a call that sent different messages to their hearts as they were scared of what the king would do to them for staying all day and not having a good reason to use as their excuse.

The weather was quite cool, even the tension that was once at the palace was now down as the people were exhausted for having waiting for Zizo the whole day without eating or drinking. Like a flash of strength entered into them when the guards started coming into the compound that housed King Katinu. They all stood up at same time waiting for Zizo and his baby to come into the compound, and when they did not see him, they turned their gaze at the king. The king asked the first guards the where about of Zizo and the unknown creature the people said they saw him with. They could not answer as they were scared, not knowing what to say. But when the guards saw that their silence was beginning to kindle the king's anger, they stammered, all saying same thing which made it impossible for everyone not to hear what they were saying. The chief priest stood up from his sitting position, walked up to the guards and then placed his staff on the chest of the leader of the palace guards.

"Now tell us what happened" Said the chief priest as he returned to his sitting position.

"When we got to Zizo's house, we searched everywhere but did not see Zizo and the unknown creature, we waited all day hoping he would return but he never did. We were scared of returning to the palace because my king ordered us not to return without Zizo and the unknown creature. However, we saw a grave at the backyard of Zizo's house, it is a newly dug grave." Said the guard in a shaky voice.

Everyone exclaimed as he spoke and when he was done narrating what happened at Zizo's place, the people grumbled but this time, the king could hear what they were saying.

"My people, please be patient and return home, you know you all are already exhausted and needed to have some rest else you start falling down and only the gods know what would follow that after. I promise you that Zizo will be brought to the palace as soon as he steps his feet into this village of ours. Go home and get some things for your stomach." King Katinu said with frown boldly written on his face.

The people upon hearing this, started leaving the palace one after the other. And when there was no one in the palace except for the chief priest, king Katinu asked him for advice on how to go about the issue that was on ground.

"My king, the issue at hand is a complicating one that needs lots of wisdom to execute else one will offend the gods. My king, I sense danger!" Said the chief priest taking his staff in his hand and then getting up from the ground. "Let Zizo be seen first, then we'll take it up from there."

11

Zizo and the baby walked about the enchanting environment of Gayu with Zizo showing him the fancy things that were in the environment.

"What happened to you baby? You do not seem to be happy or do not you like it here?" Zizo asked after sensing his baby was not saying a word on everything he saw.

The baby told him that the place was the ugliest place he had ever set his eyes on, that he preferred spending his entire life in the village than spend a day in this messy place. as he spoke, Zizo looked down on him with surprise and then noticed that the places treaded upon by the baby had turned into something that looked like they have been dead for so long a time. He did not ask the baby what that meant because he already knew. He just pretended not to have seen a thing.

"Do not worry dear; I am going to show you the fountain that has glassy waters and the ball in the cloud that looks like the moon that shines all day, lightening the environment. You will like it there and in no time, the fireflies and shinning creatures will start flying out from the ball. Your mama would say, they are the guardian of the environment." Said Zizo as he lifted the baby and then headed for the path that led to the other side of the environment.

As he walked, he turned back to have another glance of the paths that have turned into dead paths, but to his surprise, the paths have all turned back into the way they were before the baby walked on them.

"Son, you just get better but confusing by every second." Zizo thought aloud but denied he said a thing when the baby asked him what he said.

When they got to the environment, the moon-like object was shining like never before and they were fireflies and shinning creatures everywhere. He looked up and saw the ball in the cloud that looked like a moon. He told his son to look up and then showed the son the cloud that he was talking about. as they were looking at it, the thought of how him and his wife always looked at the cloud, and the fun they had together came to his mind. Tear drops came out of his eyes and he turned his attention to his son. His son asked him what the problem was but he said nothing, then he caught a firefly and showed his son.

"Wow! It shines!" His son said with a smiling face as he watched Zizo set free the firefly and it flew to join the others.

His son in joy jumped up and tried to catch one too but he could not. he tried over and over again but he could not, then Zizo carried him on his shoulder so he could catch a firefly himself. It worked as Zizo's son while on Zizo's shoulder, caught a firefly. In joy, he showed it to his father and they smiled at each other. Then he released the firefly he caught as well with smile written all over his face.

"I know you will like this place, come, let us go and have a touch of the glassy water." Zizo said with a smile on his face, he never knew that he would ever do something or show his baby a place that would make him smile the way he did.

In excitement, they left the spot and then went to the fountain that has glassy waters. On getting to the base of the fountain, Zizo made his baby sit on a stone that was not far from where the water was floating through. Zizo dipped his hand into the water and after some seconds, fetched it and used it to wash his face. Immediately he did this, his face shined brightly and he looked refreshed. his son was surprised, he asked his father if the water performed magic. Zizo told him that consoles any pure hearted person that is either troubled or sad; that the water does not like seeing good people troubled in their hearts. He told him that it was the glassy water he settled the disputes he had with Gayu.

"Come and have a feel of the water, son" Said Zizo as he again dipped his hand into the water.

In excitement, the baby stood up and rushed to where Zizo was squatting, just as he dipped his hand into the water, the water started turning into black. He became scared and he removed his hands.

Zizo was surprised at what happened, he looked at the baby with surprise look, "What kind of mysterious child is this that even the glassy water rejected him" Zizo soliloquized but then gave a smiling face so his baby would not feel bad or ask him questions.

He encouraged his baby to give it another try, but as his baby did, the water again started turning into black and this angered the baby, he left the water and then walked back with folded arms, to the stone where he was sitting. Zizo went to meet him, squatting in front of him, he told his son not to get angry because the water turned black when he dipped his hand into the water.

He told him that the water must have been angered by the gods, "We shall come here tomorrow."

He made some funny looks at the baby that made him laugh.

"Come, let us go to your mom's house." Zizo said, standing up, holding his baby by the hand, he led him out of the environment.

At night while Zizo was asleep in Gayu's house, Ghoulbraham got up and went to where the glassy water was, he dipped his hands into it and again it turned to black, he became so furious that he refused to remove his hand from the water then suddenly the water dried up. He looked at his hands in surprise and then ran back to sleep.

The following morning while Zizo was still asleep, Ghoulbraham woke him up, asking they return to Inoko.

"But son, remember I told you we will be visiting the fountain today." Zizo said rubbing his eyes with the back of his palm. Ghoilbraham told him he was no longer interested in the fountain, that they should go to Inoko that they never planned for would happen. Zizo was about declining his request when he remembered the advice of the aged woman that says he should always do Ghoulbraham's wishes. He sighed and then told Ghoulbraham to hold on while he fixed some things before they would return to Inoko. Ghoulbraham grinned and for the first time since he was born, he told Ziizo that he loved him.

The sun was yet to come out of its hiding place in the cloud when Zizo and Ghoulbraham came out from the pathway that led to the enchanting world. Zizo smiled but soon wore a frown on his face as he pointed to the stream that was at the other end. He told Ghoulbraham that years back before he met Gayu, he and his beloved friend bathed in the stream.

"As a matter of fact, we were both in this stream when I first heard the flute of your mother emanating from this part." Said Zizo pointing to the pathway from which they came out from. "We grew up together, worked in our farms together, ate together and did almost everything together with smiling faces. He was a good friend until he fell ill and one day, saw me with your mother. Till date, I am yet to know what actually made him change his once kind attitude towards me, and what..." Zizo was still talking when Ghoulbraham told him he knew about Tuna and how he died.

"You do?" Zizo said as he bent to look into Ghoulbraham's mouth as if to bring out the answer from it.

Ghoulbraham smiled and gave out a wicked laugh. He told Zizo that it was Tuna's father that actually turned Tuna against him.

"He also asked his servants not to allow you in when you wanted to check on him." Ghoulbraham spoke as Zizo paid all his attention to him like someone that is receiving lectures from his instructor.

Ghoulbraham told him that he believed Tuna was killed because he refused to listen to the warnings of the gods... people that die mysteriously are people that never obey the gods.

"It was not the gods that killed Tuna's papa but Tuna himself." Ghoulbraham said as he placed his hands on Zizo's shoulders.

Zizo was confused about this particular part of the story, he asked for clarification as an already dead man could not have killed another, not to talk about one that so loved his father while alive. Ghoulbraham told him that the spirit of Tuna was not happy with his father because he was showed all the atrocities of his father and how his father had tricked him into believing what was not.

"His spirit became jealous seeing his papa living while he that wanted to explore the world labored in tears at the other side of the great curtain that separates the living from the dead." Ghoulbraham said now removing his hands from Zizo's shoulders.

Zizo was perplexed at Ghoulbraham but dared not ask him how he got to know about things that happened while he was yet to be born.

"Let us start going before someone will see us standing at this junction and wonder what we are doing here." Said Zizo as he carried Ghoulbraham up, placed him on his shoulder and then journeyed home with him holding Ghoulbraham's feet so he would not fall from his shoulder.

As they walk home, they met some people who screamed and then ran away to a place neither Zizo nor Ghoulbraham knew. Although Zizo did not know the reason behind their running away, however, he told Ghoulbraham not to wonder or worry about them.

"Do you know what I am thinking about?" Zizo asked Ghoulbraham who shook his head.

Zizo told him he was thinking of what he would feed him when they get home. Ghoulbraham cackled, he reminded Zizo of the meal he prepared the night before they left for the aged woman's place.At this, Zizo was relieved.

"Please hurry up papa, I am so hungry." Ghoulbraham said rubbing his stomach.

"Yes, my lord!" Zizo said with smiling face and then hastened his footsteps.

12

The sun was yet to come out from the cloud and King Katinu was enjoying his sleep when he woke up to a sudden sound that seemed as if people were fighting in his palace. Quickly he got up from his bed, grabbed his weapon and then dashed out of his room. He was a bit disappointed but gave a sigh of relief when he came out and saw it was not the sound of war but the sound of some of his subjects. When they saw him, they became scared because of the weapon he was holding and all kept quiet and never said a thing until he commanded them to. They told him Zizo and the creature was in the village. He asked them if they were sure about what they told him and they all chorused yes. At this, he sent some guards to fetch Zizo and the creature, and then sent another set of guards to fetch the chief priest. He asked the people to go home and return in the noon when he would question Zizo after he must have fixed some things in the palace, but the people refused going and returning in the noon, they said they would stay back at the palace until everything was done.

"Please yourself but make sure you do not start that continue that sound of yours." King Katinu said as he returns to his chamber.

The people were troubled at heart but never dared saying another word in the palace.

***

The sun rose on Zizo feeding Ghoulbraham with the rotten meal at home. The meal had bad smell but Ghoulbraham loved it. Even though its smell made Zizo cover his nostrils and mouth with one of his hands, Ghoulbraham ate it with smiles all over his face.

"Tell me, why do you like eating rotten meals son?" Zizo tried to speak from his covered mouth.

Ghoulbraham told him that he ate rotten meals because they strengthen his body and make him be who he was.

"If I do not eat rotten meals, there will be no fresh meal in this world of yours; remember, it takes a life to bring a life." Said Ghoulbraham after swallowing the meal in his mouth.

Zizo was about asking another question when the guards that were sent arrived his place. They asked him to follow them to the palace as the king needed to ask him some questions.

"So, you now talk to me? I thought all of you are under the decree that says none should talk to me or my household why I live in this village?" Zizo said getting up from the seat he sat while feeding Ghoulbraham.

"Come of it Zizo! The maker of the decree is the same one that has asked we bring you to the palace for questioning." One of the guards spoke.

"Now, I want you to go back to the king and tell him I am not coming to his palace. he cannot be using me as a puppet. He made my family and I suffer for many years in isolation, and now he calls me to his palace? Well, I was feeding my son before you all walked in, so I ask you allow me continue with that." Zizo said staring at the faces of the guards.

Like a flash of lightening, one of the guards got a hold of Ghoulbraham, placing his weapon at him, he ordered Zizo to follow the others else he would kill Ghoulbraham.

"Please do not kill me." Ghoulbraham begged the guard.

Zizo looked at Ghoulbraham and saw the look of helplessness in his eyes. He asked the guard that was holding Ghoulbraham to please let him go, as he was ready to follow them to the palace. The guard dropped Ghoulbraham on the floor and Ghoulbraham ran to one end of the house. The guard asked the other guards to move Zizo out of the compound.

"Are we not carrying the baby as well?" one of the guards asked the guard that seemed to be their leader, the same guard that once held Ghoulbraham and gave them the order to take Zizo away.

"The king asked we get Zizo, not this unknown thing here." Said the guard pointing at Ghoulbraham.

At this, Zizo was relieved. He asked they allow him take Ghoulbraham inside his room before taking him to King Katinu but his request was not granted. They pushed him out of the compound with Ghoulbraham watching helplessly.

"Why do I feel as if something is missing inside of me? I want to do some things but cannot." Ghoulbraham said taking his bowl of meal in his hands and looking at the direction, they went out from.

There was great jubilation at the palace as the guards that were sent to get Zizo arrived the palace with Zizo, even the chief priest was relieved as he now wore a smiling face. King Katinu stood up from his chair.

"People of Inoko, the one whom we have been expecting is in our midst today. we hope we get all the answers we need from him." King Katinu said with outstretched hands and the people responded with cheers.

The king turned at Zizo, he asked him the whereabout of his wife Gayu. And after hearing she was no more; he showed no sign of pity for Zizo. He asked Zizo how she died, Zizo told him she died while giving birth to their son, but he refused telling him what actually led to her death, and this made the king and chief priest suspicious.

"The people said they saw you carrying a wrapped thing on your head and a greenish creature with three eyes on your back the day it rained heavily in this land, how true is this?" King Katinu asked Zizo as he returned to his seat.

Zizo told him it was the corpse of his wife Gayu that he carried on his head and that the creature he carried on his back was his son.

"I am very sure you killed your wife. That perfectly describes why it rained heavily on that day." King Katinu said picking up one of the fruits that were on a tray set before him.

Zizo told him he did not kill his wife, that the gods can bear him witness to that. When the people heard Zizo invoking the gods to bear witness to what he was saying, they believed him. After some seconds of silence at the palace, the king asked the where about of his baby, that he would like to see him and that it was not good leaving a newly born baby alone at home.

"My lord, there is no newly born baby in his house." The leader of the guards that they were sent to fetch Zizo spoke. "When we got there, we saw him feeding a three-eyed greenish creature with rotten meal and the creature was eating it with smiles all over its face. This creature does not look like a newly born but one that had seen some weeks."

King Kitanu asked them why didn't they bring the child along with them. The leader replied again that it was because the king asked them to bring just Zizo and not both of them. Then Zizo asked the king what does he wants to do with his son. The king replied that he just wanted to see this son, but deep down in him he wanted to kill the creature. He asked Zizo why did he decide to train that kind of creature that eats only rotten foods. Zizo replied and told him that he should stop calling his son a creature, and the king said to him that and what if he continues to call him a creature what is Zizo going to do. Zizo stared at him with an angry face but kept quiet. Then the king asked the whereabout of his son, Zizo refused to tell him. He asked again but Zizo kept quiet, the king became angry, he got up from his seat and walked to Zizo and asked him again but yet Zizo kept quiet. King Katinu smacked him on the face, then he told his guards to go to Zizo's house and search again for Ghoulbraham.

He ordered the child's execution should they find him. Zizo pleaded with the king not to kill his son, but the king refused. He ordered the guards to lock Zizo in their prison before going to search for his son. As the guards were taking Zizo away he forcefully removed his hands from theirs and ran away. The king ordered the guards to get him and kill him. Zizo ran to his house with the guards chasing him, he got to his house before the guards. On getting there, his son ran out to meet him and asked him what was going on. He did not say anything instead he carried his son, went to the balcony and put him at the base of the tree. He asked his son to climb as far as he could climb. He came out, took his sword and waited for the guards, when the guards came, he engaged them to a fight, he killed one but unfortunately for him the other ones defeated him and killed him, when all these were going on his son watched from the tree.

After killing him, they searched all over for his son but they could not find him so they left. After some time, Ghoulbraham came down from the tree and in tears ran to the spot where the body of his father was, on getting there, he saw that the father was dead, he was bitter and vowed to take revenge. He ran away into the enchanting forest. When he got to the enchanting forest, he was weak and decided to relax for some time. As he was relaxing, he felt lonely because his father was no more, but the memories of his father was with him. The flash of how his father was killed came into his mind and as he was thinking about it, a firefly flew passed him, then he remembered what his father told him about fireflies. He went to the place that was full of fireflies; he sat down there and was watching the fireflies as they flew. After sometime he became hungry, then he went in search for food, being that in the enchanting forest everywhere was neat, he could hardly find something to eat, after wandering around looking for food and couldn't find any, he was frustrated and went back to the place where fire flies were and started eating them. After eating to his satisfaction, he slept there until the next day.

***

The next morning, he woke up smiling, thinking that his father was beside him. He smiled and turned to his side but saw no one. Then he remembered that his father was dead; he became sober again and accepted his fate the way it was. He then decided to go to the glassy waters, the place he dried with his hands, on getting there. He sat down there and wished that the water was there to console him, but the place has dried up. He left and went back to the place where he saw fireflies. When he got there, he ate all the fireflies and was still hungry, he thought of other places where he could get food to eat around the enchanting forest but no idea came because the environment of the enchanting forest was neat and he did not like a neat environment.

Then the idea of going to the stinky forbidden forest came to his mind, he feared the fact that no one has ever gone into the forbidden forest alone and then come out of it alive except when they went in to drop a corpse that desecrated the land when he as alive. Not wanting to risk his life, Ghoulbraham wandered the around the forest for days. One day, as he was wandering round the forest, he saw some palace guards who upon seeing him, started walking toward his direction. Not knowing what to do and where to run to, he ran into the forbidden forest. He did not stop running until he was deep into the forest. He turned his back but did not see any of the guards. The guards had stopped chasing him because they knew that he would not last the night.

Ghoulbraham turned to have a look at the forest from the spot he was standing. Everywhere was messy; it was as if the trees had a fight with themselves. The air in this place was polluted with smell of dead animals. He was at the heart of the forest where they usually dropped the bodies of the people that desecrated the land. He looked around but did not see any dead body. As he turned, his eyes caught the sight of carcasses of dead animals around. He rushed to the first animal he saw and then devoured it like he was going to die the next minute.

"Never knew a place like this exist in Inoko." Ghoulbraham soliloquized as he takes another bite from the meat.

"Serves him right, let him go into the forbidden forest and die there." Said the leader of the guards that saw Ghoulbraham and then chased him into the forbidden forest.

"And we thought he has long left this village or probably must have died of starvation after he ran the other day." Another guard said, gasping for breath.

The leader of the guards asked they return to the palace and tell the king who they saw wondering in the village and how they had chased him into the forbidden forest.

13

King Katinu was enjoying his afternoon with the chief priest feasting on the dishes that were served him and the chief priest when the guards returned to inform him of who they saw in the village and how they had chased him into the forbidden forest. King Katinu was shocked at hearing that Ghoulbraham was still alive and well. He looked at the chief priest and then gave a cruel laugh. He turned back at the guards, he informed them to mount guard at the entrance of the forest and never to let him live else they would have to pay dearly for it with their lives. He called the palace messenger, and then asked him to announce to the village that Ghoulbraham has been banished from the land and on the wanted list, that anyone that saw him should kill him and get an awesome reward from the palace.

"Does the anyone also include us, my lord?" One of the palace guards asked as the messenger ran off to deliver the king's message to the people.

"Yes, everyone including the chief priest that is sitting here with me. And if it happens to be an animal that kills him, the animal will be fatted for years until it dies a natural death. And when this happens, it will be giving a ceremonious burial."

The guards including the chief priest opened their mouth at the proclamation of the king. The king smiled and returned to his seat, leaving the guards and chief priest to fantasize on what he had said. The guards looked at each other and then ran off to carry out the king's order. Even the chief priest wanted to leave the palace as well to commence on his quest to finding and killing Ghoulbraham, but King Katinu stopped him, asking he finishes the meal that was before them.

"My king, this is the right and best hour to kill that creature because he is yet to have a full knowledge of who he is and the powers he possesses. I do not want it to slip through our fingers because if he does, we all including the village are doomed." Said the chief priest as he took a bite from the meal that was in his left hand.

King Katinu smiled at this, he told the chief priest not to be in a haste but enjoyed his meal because he would always get the baby to kill as he was just a kid and would not understand the tactics of staying away from invaders.

"I trust your magical powers; I am very sure your magical powers would lead you to him and destroy him before anyone can." King Katinu said after taking a sip from the liquid bottle that was in front of him.

As the message of the king reached the people of Inoko through the king's messenger, more than half of the people in Inoko especially the lazy ones that were after quick riches, headed for the forbidden forest. They paid deaf ears to the pleading of their loved ones who pleaded they should not go into the forbidden forest as no one ever survived it there not talking about spending a night in the forest. The ones that did not go to the forest were on a look out for Ghoulbraham should he come out of the forest at night or at any hour to get water or food.

***

Before the moon would come out from the cloud, the in and out of the forbidden forest were like the king's palace when the village was celebrating an important feast. It was so rowdy that people had to fight for who would go into the forest and who would not. The guards and some people entered into the forest all fully armed with clubs and swords. Some of them carried halogen lamp should it get dark and Ghoulbraham was yet to be seen and killed.

Ghoulbraham was eating the body of a dead animal and was enjoying himself when he became thirsty. He looked around but did not see water. He searched the part of the forest he was staying in for water but still did not see water. He resorted to the nasty fluid that was in the intestine of the animal he was feeding on, lucky for him, the rain that fell some days back was still inside the punctured part of the animal. He scooped the water with his hands, though the water he scooped was much, only little of it entered into his mouth. He sucked the fluid in the intestine of the animal he fed on but again, the fluid was not enough. He thought for a moment and then recalled his father telling him about how some trees have water inside their branches.

On the other side the when the people got to the forest, they decided to divide themselves so as to catch Ghoulbraham where ever he is hiding and also because they don't want to share the reward that the king would give to them, some went to the other side of the forest, while others took their own positions. Ghoulbraham then climbed the tree, on climbing the tree; he took one branch of the tree and checked if there was water in it, when he found out that there is water inside the branch, he became happy because he was not satisfied with the water he got from the intestine of the animal. He sucked the first one but still was not satisfied, he drank almost all the water in all the branches but was not satisfied. It was just one branch left that one was a little bit far from the rest branches. He went for the last branch and as he was about sucking the water from the branch, a bee stung him. As he was trying to kill the bee, he saw something that looked like a creature, he decided to take a close look to see who the creature was, when he looked closely, he found out that the creature dressed like the guards that came to his father's house when was young. After accessing their regalia, he found out that it was the people from the Inoko village.

"What are these people doing in the forest, I thought no one dared to enter the forbidden forest?" Ghoulbraham said holding a tree branch.

He heard one telling the other that he would be the one to catch the little creature and claim the king's reward. And the other told the first one that he could do anything to the little creature just to claim the reward. Ghoulbraham hurriedly climbed down from the tree and thought of what he could do to save himself but no idea came into his mind. He became even more terrified because the people were coming closer to him and also, they were bigger than him. He was frustrated and sat down crying and saying to himself that his life was over, while he was saying these words, the spirit of his late father appeared to him and told him not to worry, that he should gather the carcass of the dead animal he ate, and after gathering them he should lie down under it so that the people would not know that he is there.

So, he did as he was told and laid down under the carcass of the dead animal, after doing this, a big snake came out from a tree closer to the tree Ghoulbraham climbed on, the snake glided to the place where the people were, it mixed itself with the leaves and prepared itself to kill. One of the people was almost getting to the place where Ghoulbraham was when he stepped on the leaves that were covering the snake and immediately the snake killed that one and then went to another place to take position. It climbed another tree and waited, unfortunately another one was tired and decided to rest on a tree, unknowingly to the creature that the snake was there, so the snake came out and again it struck. And again, it left that spot and went to another place to take position, another one was searching for Ghoulbraham when he was attacked by the same snake and died instantly.

When another passed through the same place where the previous one passed, it came across the dead body of the other one. He was surprised and thought of what would have killed the other one. He decided to inspect the body of the dead one. As he was inspecting the body of the dead one, he saw the mark of snakebites on the neck of the dead one. Then he knew that it was a snake that killed the other one. He brought out his sword and prepared himself in case the snake was there so that he would kill the snake. He looked around if he would see the snake, but he did not see any snake so he said to him that maybe the snake wasn't there, so he kept his sword and continue to search for Ghoulbraham, but just as he took a few steps forward, the snake struck him and he died.

The strongest of them all was walking on the forest in search for the little creature, he came across the same snake, the snake positioned itself on the ground, he said to himself, "I could use this snake to scare that little creature and capture him, so let me catch this snake and keep it."

He walked towards the snake and tried to capture it but he missed his target and the snake struck him, the man died on the spot. When the sun was setting two people came across something that looked like Ghoulbraham, when they saw it, they started dragging who will capture the little creature. Meanwhile another guard was at the corner watching them. He was waiting for one to kill the other before he would attack and killed him. While they were dragging, one pushed the other on the ground and as he was about to grab the thing that looked like the little creature, the one on the ground stood up quickly and struck the other one with his sword and killed him. After killing the first one as he was about grabbing the thing that looked like the little creature, the other guard that was watching at the corner came out and struck him on his head with a big wood. The guard died and then the guard that killed the other guard grabbed the thing that looked like Ghoulbraham. He found out that it was not Ghoulbraham it was just a stick that formed something like Ghoulbraham. He was so disappointed and walked away. The chief priest searched for the little creature but could not find the creature as well, even he was interested because of the reward from the king and so he killed the guards that came crossed his path while he was searching for the little creature.

When night came some of the people in the forest, especially the women, decided to take some rest due to tiredness, this gave the snake an opportunity to kill even more. One of the women who was sleeping woke up to go and urinate, so she went to another place in the forest to urinate and as she was urinating, the snake struck her there and she died. Another was sleeping with her husband when her husband rolled away from the spot where he was. This gave the snake an opportunity to glide into the spot where the man was. The woman placed her hand on the snake thinking it was her husband, suddenly she noticed that her hand was cold, she opened her eyes and saw that it was snake she laid her hand on. Just as she screamed, the snake struck her, it struck her husband as well and left. On the other side of the forbidden forest two men were using their halogen lamp to look for Ghoulbraham. They got to a spot that had wooden bridge that was not stable. At the end of the bridge, they saw a shadow that looked like that of Ghoulbraham. Because it was night, there could not see it properly, so both of them began to cross the bridge and as they crossed, they fought on who would get the creature and because of this, the bridge broke and both of them fell into a hole and they died.

14

When it was morning, the people discovered that majority of them where dead, so the remaining ones ran out of the forest because they were afraid of death including the chief priest. Then the snake glided to where Ghoulbraham was. It turned into the spirit of his mother, and then that of his father appeared too and they told him to come out from his hiding. Ghoulbraham came out and they told him again not to worry that they were going to help him, in fear he asked them how they are going to help him.

"It is true that you are on a mission to bringing justice to the oppressed, but one thing you do not know is that we are part of that mission... you need us to complete that mission." Gayu's spirit said walking towards Ghoulbraham.

"There are so many things about yourself that you do not know son, and we have been asked by our keeper to guard you until you are ripe for the tasks that are ahead of you." Zizo's spirit said still standing at the spot it was when it appeared.

"I wish I know more about me!" Ghoulbraham said with blue tears coming down his eyes.

Patting Ghoulbraham's head, Gayu told him that he should not worry about that as they were going to leave him a parting gift that would keep him safe and make his inability of knowing more about himself to be a thing that he would give little attention to. Ghoulbraham asked Gayu what she meant and how that was going to be possible. Just then, the spirit of Zizo walked up to the spot where Gayu and Ghoulbraham were standing. He gave Ghoulbrahmn a smile, placed his right hand on Ghoulbraham's shoulder and then vanished into him. Ghoulbraham looked around but did not see Zizo's spirit, he called out to him but there was no response. Turning to asked Gayu the where about of Zizo's spirit, Gayu's spirit vanished into him and there was a thunder blast.

"Papa! Mama!" Ghoulbraham called out in aches, calling them to come and keep him company but there was no reply.

He knelt down in aches to cry but tear drops never came down from his eyes. He wondered why because he was feeling himself crying but there was no teardrop that was coming down his cheeks. He forced himself to cry but this time around, the blood color that was coming out of his eyes turned to black color. He wondered what was happening to him. While he was still wondering what was happening to him, a big tree cracked and then fell, instead of hitting Ghoulbraham, it fell through him, it was as if Ghoulbraham was air. Ghoulbraham looked at the part of the tree that was behind him and the part that was in front of him and then to himself but still did not understand there was a transformation somewhere. He walked on the log still wondering what had happened.

"Why would I die when I am yet to complete my assignment?" Ghoulbraham said putting one of his index fingers into his mouth.

As he walked on the log of wood, his eyes caught a glimpse of a rotten animal hanging on the branch of the tree that was in front of him. He hurriedly jumped down from the fallen log and then hurriedly climbed the tree to get the rotten animal. Unfortunately, as Ghoulbraham was about getting hold of the animal, the branch of the tree on which the animal and Ghoulbraham were on, broke and Ghoulbraham fell to the ground. it was a hard fall, but Ghoulbraham had no injury.

"So, I am now invisible!" Ghoulbraham said with a smile as he uses his hand to clean his body.

"You are not invisible, but you can become invisible by just saying a word." Gayu's voice spoke from the inside of Ghoulbraham.

At the palace, the king was told all that had happened in the forbidden forest. He was furious about what he heard yet wonder if Ghoulbraham had anything to do with the snake that attacked them in the forest. He sent for the chief priest but was told that the chief priest was seriously not himself but down with heavy heart as he too did not believe what he saw in the forest. King Katinu was perplexed, he asked the guard he inquired from the guard he was talking to if there were still people in front of the forest. And when he got a positive answer from him, he called on his palace messenger and then sent him to the people living in the village especially the ones that were in front of the forest to tell them that he just doubled the bounty on Ghoulbraham's head. He told them that if anyone should kill Ghoulbraham, the kingdom would be divided into two factions and when he dies, that lucky person would be the one to rule the both villagers.

"My King are you sure of what you are saying? How can you make such promise knowing that as the king of this village it is forbidden to go back on your word after it has reached the hearing of the people? Okay, my king, if you do mean what you have said, what would be the fate of the chief priest who ought to take after you after your demise?" The guard King Katinu was first talking to before the coming of the palace messenger asked King Katinu.

King Katinu sent the palace messenger away to deliver his message. He then told the guard that he meant what he had said as he was very sure if anyone can kill Ghoulbraham, it would be the Chief Priest because he alone has the spiritual powers that would link him to Ghoulbraham and then bring to life his dream.

"You know it will not be a bad thing if the chief priest should take after me as he has been faithful to me and only him has the capabilities of ruling this kingdom rightly, taking it to a better level. More so, since death of my wife, he has been almost everything to me." King Katinu said with a smiling face as he returns into his chamber, leaving the guard to wonder in deep thought.

The guard bowed and then walked out of King Katinu's palace, promising himself to be the one that would catch and kill Ghoulbraham.

***

The messenger got to the chief priest's house where he met him deep with thoughts with his right hand under his chin. The incident that happened the previous night was still a shocker to him. He was pondering on how he had managed to survive and what made him and others unable to catch Ghoulbraham in the forest. The messenger called him several times but he did not notice his presence. He called again and when he saw there was no change, he moved to tap the chief priest on his shoulder but was stopped by an unknown force. The chief priest turned his head at his direction with his eyes red like burning cools. He asked the palace messenger what had brought him to his abode at an hour he did not want to share with anyone. The messenger in fright apologized for his intrusion, and when he was satisfied by his plea, he delivered King Katinu's message to the chief priest.

"Are you sure of the things you just said?" Asked the chief priest.

"Yes, I am, and I know our king meant every bit of what I told you." the messenger replied. The chief priest stood up with mixed feelings of rage and joy in his heart. he grabbed his staff and after swinging it in the air, asked the messenger to tell the king that he should expect to receive the head of Ghoulbraham before the end of that day. The messenger bowed and then left the chief priest with question like how was the chief priest going to bring his promise to life in his mind but dared not ask him because of the nature of his eyes and how he spoke in rage.

When the people in the forest got the information too, they became jealous of the chief priest because somehow, they got to know that King Katinu actually made those pronouncements because of the chief priest. They did not allow their jealousy get the better part of them, but motivate them so they too can rule over Inoko someday. Though they were motivated by the words of the king, none dares going into the forest to search for Ghoulbraham as some of them were witnesses to what happened in the forest.

They waited all day for Ghoulbraham to come out but he never did. Some of them became discouraged, they went home having the believe that it was not in their stars to kill Ghoulbraham. As they were leaving with their heads facing the ground, the brave ones came together to plan what should be done so they would not end up like the lazy ones that were leaving. They were still on their plan when a rush of wind blew pass them and then into the forest. They wondered what the wind meant. Though they were bold, they were not bold enough to enter into it as the rush of wind could be the spirit of one of the people that were buried in the forest. What they did not know was that the wind was not the spirit of any dead person, but the chief priest using his magical powers so he would not be hurt by Ghoulbraham. They decided to wait until morning before they would go inside the forest to scout for Ghoulbraham.

***

By now, Ghoulbraham was no longer the way he was when he ran back into the forest the noon of the previous day. He now looked someone that was seven years old. Just as Ghoulbraham looked around for dead animals but there was none in sight. He searched the forest but there was no decaying animal in every part of the forest. Putting his hands on his waist, he thought of what he would do. While he was still in his thought, he smelt the smell of garbage and then sniffed to where it was. To his surprise, there was a can of debris before him. it was as if some people had visited that part of the forest before he even ventured into the forest.

Although the garbage smelt horribly, he loved it because it was just in the perfect state he needed it to be in. He gave a smile that lasted for some seconds before proceeding to devour the garbage. He had no need for water as he had already got some from one of the trees that produced water from its branches. While Ghoulbraham was enjoying his meal, he heard the sound of a mighty wind rushing towards his direction. He quickly grabbed the garbage he could grab but before he would wish to be invincible, the mighty wind was already in front of it, without wasting time, it flung Ghoulbraham into the air. And before Ghoulbraham would regain himself and then make the wish of becoming invincible, the wind flung him again into the air and this time, Ghoulbraham landed on his stomach and it hurt him a lot.

He sensed the wind was no normal wind that someone or some forces were behind it. Gasping for breath, he asked whomever that was behind the wind to reveal himself. He was still on it when a familiar voice came out from the wind and in no time, the wind transformed into the chief priest. Ghoulbraham asked him why he and the people of Inoko wanted him dead but the chief priest gave him no reply but walked towards him.

"You survived the previous night, and have been surviving all attempts to kill you, but today, you will not survive it." Said the chief priest as he was now very close to Ghoulbraham who was by now laying helplessly on the ground. "A huge bounty has been put on your head by the king and everyone is now on your trail, all want to be the lucky winner that will rule after the death of king Katinu. Too bad no one but I can attain the bounty. I will make your death swift, will not let you suffer the way your father and grandparents survived and begged for life. And after killing you and taking your head to king Katinu and he crowned me the next in line of king-ship, I shall kill him." Said the chief priest as he raised Ghoulbraham up with his left hand, and lifting up his staff to stab Ghoulbraham, Ghoulbraham vanished from his hand.

He was surprised as he never thought someone like Ghoulbra-ham who was yet to know much about himself and the power he possessed could vanish. He called on Ghoulbraham to come out from his hiding, saying it was only cowards that hide their identities when fighting.

"How dare you call me a coward?" Ghoulbraham said ripping out the chief priest's intestine a second after his appearance, not giving the chief priest anytime to act. "You now call me a coward! Calling me a coward means that you are equally a bigger coward because you never attacked me in your real identity. I am the gods' punish-ment on anyone that is not true to himself." Said Ghoulbraham as the chief priest struggle to breathe.

Wanting to strike Ghoulbraham with his staff, Ghoulbraham vanished but appeared again slicing the throat of the chief priest with his long fingernails.

"I hate cowards and people who disrespect the gods." Ghoulbra-ham said as the chief priest dropped down dead.

Confirming the chief priest was dead, Ghoulbraham walked to the trash he was feasting on before the chief priest attacked him. he pulled out a waste whistling as he ate it.

**

The evening was a long but nice one for the people that were outside the forbidden forest. They all slept like warriors who had just returned from a fierce battle. On the other hand, King Katinu slept and dreamt. In his dream, he saw the chief priest presenting the head of Ghoulbraham to him, and there was a great celebration in Inoko. He smiled as he dreamt.

It was morning the following day; the trees in and around the forest were beginning to wake up when the people that kept watch on the forbidden forest woke up to the greatest surprise of their lives. They woke up and saw the corpse of the chief priest in their midst. What baffled them mostly was how the body of the chief priest was deposited in their midst and none of them knew when it happened or who dropped it in their midst. they were so scared that none dared to carry the body into the village. Like a bombshell was dropped in their midst, they all ran away in different directions, leaving the body to be bathed by the early morning dew.

15

King Katinu was still enjoying his sleep when he heard people shouting in his palace. He jumped out from his bed wearing a smiling face as he thought that his dream had become reality. He quickly got himself into his favorite royal attire as he usually did whenever there was an important occasion in the community. He smiled as he adjusted himself in front of a mirror he brought out from his wardrobe. Feeling satisfied, he walked out of his chamber with thoughts of how many days he was going to celebrate the good news and how many houses he was going to give to the lucky one that brought his dream into life.

Instead of seeing smiling faces in his compound, he was greeted by the tears of people who cried as if they had been flogged by the gods. He was surprised at what he was seeing. He called them to inquire the reason why they were weeping but they ignored him like they always did whenever there was a serious issue in the village.

King Katinu was disturbed, he called on one of his guard and then ordered him to bring out one of the people that was weeping. When this was done, King Katinu ordered the guard to kill the person he brought out if he should ignore his question.

"Now tell me, why are you people wailing like newly born babies?" King Katinu asked the person that was held by the guard.

The person still did not say a word. This made king Katinu so vexed that he pulled out a sword from the sheath the guard that was closed to him was carrying. He raised it up and just as he was about bringing it down on the person, one of the people told him there would not be any need of sharing another blood because the only one that would have interceded on their behalf to the gods should they get angry at the death, was no more.

"What did you just say?" King Katinu asked with the sword still in the air.

"We do not know how it happened or who did it my lord. We woke up to see the disfigured body of our chief priest in front of the palace. So my king, I think you should think twice before bringing down the sword on an innocent man who has lost his mind due to what happened yesterday and what he says today." The man said wiping his eyes with the back of his palm.

Slowly, king Katinu brought down the sword he was holding, he asked the man who spoke the where about of the corpse. After he was told, he ordered the guards to fetch it and then ordered they give it a befitting funeral, which was against the tradition of the people. it was a tradition that anyone that was ripped open by anyone should not be buried but thrown into the forbidden forest. Although the people of Inoko knew it was forbidden to bury the chief priest, they did not object, as they were all scared of who would take the body into the forbidden forest.

**

There was total sadness in Inoko as the chief priest was laid to rest in a grand style as ordered by King Katinu who was the most heartbroken amongst the people not because the chief priest was a well-respected personality, but because he was the one, he shared his deepest secrets with, and the one he perpetrated evil with. The king declared two days of mourning for the chief priest instructing everyone not to go their farms or stream, not to go out and not to visit each other.

It was already evening and the second day of mourning. The stars were beginning to twinkle brightly in the sky, Ghoulbraham walked the forest searching for decaying things he could feed on but did not see any. As he decided to explore the other part of the forest, he noticed that section was quiet, it was that part of the forest that people do come in through whenever they have something to do in the forest. He wondered why because that place in the previous days had been noisy and busy with people walking up and down, waiting for him to come out so they could kill him. Although Ghoulbraham could vanish, he dared not try his disappearing strength out there because while trying to outsmart one, another would attack him from behind. He climbed up the tree that was close to the entrance to have a clearer view of the entrance of the forest.

As he did, he discovered there was not a single person in front of the forest. He peered through the dark night from the treetop but still did not see anyone in front of the forest and around the forest.

"And I thought the death of that cruel man would make the king and his people very mad at me! Did not know it would make them retreat. Now they have retreated and stopped chasing me, I know for sure that they would be skimming on new tactics to get at me." Ghoulbraham soliloquized from the treetop.

As he soliloquized, his stomach grumbled and that made him remember it was actually hunger that made him climb the treetop for he had not eaten for two days. From the treetop, he disappeared and appeared in front of the forest, and like a king, he walked gallantly away from the forest into the village. When he got to the village, he discovered the village that used to be lively even at night was now like a graveyard. He gave a look that seemed as if he was smiling and angry at the same time. Not wanting to be caught off guard, he quickly searched for junks in the house in front of it. He searched but did not see any junk, he searched and sniffed with his nostrils too. As he sniffed, his nostrils caught the scent of junk. He smiled and ran towards the direction the scent came from. When he got there, it was actually junk and the junk was in a can. He went closer to the junk and discovered the junk was not much.

"This will not quench my hunger but its scent is so inviting, and I am very hungry!" Ghoulbraham said staring at the junks.

Seconds later, Ghoulbraham was already inside the trashcan devouring the junk in it with a speed of light and in no time, there was no junk in the trashcan. He placed his right hand on his stomach and wanting to give a smile, his stomach grumbled again.

"I knew it was not going to fill me but..." As Ghoulbraham soliloquized, his eyes caught the sight of another trashcan, with smiling face he ran to it and soon was inside the trashcan devouring the waste that was inside. And so Ghoulbraham went all night devouring every junk he came across with until his stomach stopped grumbling. He laughed as he returned to the forest to sleep on a treetop.

***

It was morning in Inoko, a winter morning that everyone always looked forward to as it was a season when they would not suffer the scotching of the sun like they always did. This very morning was different from other mornings because there was no chipping of birds and no dancing of trees. It was so perfect that one would think that was the time nature decided to mourn the demise of the chief priest. King Katinu sat alone in his palace remembering the time spent in the chief priest's company. As he remembered, he bit his lips and allowed tears to flow freely from his eyes.

He thought about the chief priest, his mind drifted to how he would rule the people of Inoko without the guidance of the chief priest, he thought about if the gods should choose a new chief priest, he would know all his secrets and that would be the end of his reign as king of the Inoko people. King Katinu was still deep in his thoughts when some people came into his palace, all carrying their trashcans on their heads. He wondered what they were up to but quickly wiped away his tears before they would see it as it was against the traditions of the people to see the tears of the king. He stood up and walked out to meet them.

Before he would ask what the issue was, one of them spoke up. She told King Katinu that they woke up to the greatest surprise of their lives as the wastes that were in their trashcans were nowhere to be found.

"And that means one thing my king, the strange creature invaded our community last night and we know he will invade again." The oldest amongst them spoke up still carrying his trashcan on his head.

"The question is, if he should keep invading the village and keep eating all our junks, what would be our fate the day he does not see junks to eat?" Another spoke up.

King Katinu was frightened deep inside because he knew that if there are no more junks in the community, Ghoulbraham would resort to piling up people and animals until they become suitable for him to feed on. He scratched his head and then asked the people to always have junks in their trashcans until he figured out how to go about Ghoulbraham. He told them to call Ghoulbraham, Ghoul whenever they see him because he forbids it, and it was one thing he knew would help the situation at hand. He also asked them to go home and think if there was a time, their dead parents or grandparents told them a story about Ghoulbraham as that too would aid in destroying him.

He also advised they start putting poison in their junks so Ghoulbraham would eat and die. He promised that whoever could kill him through this means or any other means would be handsomely rewarded. the people looked at the king but did not say a word as they could see visible effect of what the demise of the chief priest was doing to him. They however went home discussing how to get Ghoulbraham and where to hear a story of him.

That day was like a festive day as everyone could be seen walking up and down the village asking questions about Ghoulbraham from everyone they came across with. The elderly ones were not left out as they too went in search of tales about Ghoulbraham. While they were racking their brains on that, Ghoulbraham was enjoying his sleep on the treetop. As he slept, he saw the aged woman Zizo took him to in his dream. The woman was not smiling even when he tried making her laugh.

"Master, look at what they did to me?" The aged woman said with tears of blood coming down her cheeks.

He walked up to her and when he attempted holding her hands, she disappeared. Ghoulbraham woke up from his sleep with fright written on his face. He jumped down from the tree and then disappeared to appear in the pathway that led to the aged woman's home. As he walked down the path, he looked around making sure no one was following him. When he got to the aged woman's hut, he discovered the house had long been evacuated as they were dust and cobwebs everywhere. He searched in and around the house but did not see the aged woman. At this point, Ghoulbraham became scared as the dream flashed through his mind. He wished she was safe wherever she might be. He teleported himself to many places but did not see the aged woman.

"Where could she be?" Ghoulbraham soliloquized as he walked down the path that led to the forest.

He stayed all day on the treetop in the stinking forbidden forest thinking about the aged woman and wishing she were fine wherever she might be. His thought soon made him hungry but he could not go out looking for food in the trashcan because it was still daylight and he did not know what the people had in store for him. he endured the hunger until it was late into the evening. Soon, the sun was setting and the people of Inoko were beginning to retire to their home, all looking joyful as one who had just been blessed by the gods. They were looking joyful not because they had heard stories about Ghoulbraham, but because they had injected the trashes in their trashcans with poisonous substances. The substances in their trashes were so much that it would kill anyone that tasted it within ten seconds.

They all went into their various homes believing that they would see the lifeless body of Ghoulbraham in the village. As they all retired to their homes, the only disturbing thought that was in each of their minds was who would be the lucky one that would find the lifeless body of Ghoulbraham the following day. Even King Katinu was not left out as he had instructed his servants to poison the trashes in the trashcans that were in his palace.

"Now that the sun has set and everyone has retired to their stinky homes, let me fill my stomach with some nice foods before the creatures in my stomach would eat me out." Ghoulbraham said holding his grumbling stomach as he walked out of stinky forest.

Soon, he was in the heart of Inoko. He did not bother checking the trashcans of the houses he visited the other night but went straight to other houses. What he did not know was that most of the people in the community were not sleeping, they only pretended as if they were. Ghoulbraham did not bother using his nostrils to sniff about so as to know where the trashcans were because they were placed at in front of the houses he went to.

"This people are becoming nicer than I thought! They left their trashes in front of their houses! Oh! They want the nice scent of the trashes to give their homes nice fragrance! If they should go on this way, I will not have to bring down the punishment of the gods upon them." Ghoulbraham said as he jumped into the trashcan that was before him, devouring the trash that was in it, not knowing that he was been watched by the residents of that home who was already jubilating inside, knowing that before he would finish the trash that was inside the trashcan, he would drop dead.

"Wow! That was a nice one!" Ghoulbraham said, rubbing his stomach as he walked out of the compound alive, leaving its occupants heartbroken.

He went to another house and did the same thing. That night was one of the best nights for Ghoulbraham as there was free food everywhere he went to. After eating up the meals in the trashcans he came across, he decided to have a taste of the palace's trash.

"If the people should have sumptuous meals in their cans, I wonder how the king's own would taste. Having a feel of it before morning will not be a bad idea." Ghoulbraham said and then headed straight to King Katinu's palace.

He was amazed by the sight of trashcans that were in the king's palace, it was as if the trashcans were having a match pass because they were arranged in lines of twos.

"If only I knew this is how the king's palace is, I would not have eaten the sumptuous meals of those people... now my stomach is almost filled and here before me is the most enticing meal I have ever set my eyes on." Ghoulbraham said wearing a sad face. "Well. let me get some into my stomach so my eyes can be at peace with my stomach." Ghoulbraham said as he walked towards the first two trashcans that were close to him.

In no time, he was already inside one of the trashcans and in a twinkle of an eye, he had finished up the trash in it. He gave a smile, the nicest he had even shown since his birth. He jumped into the other trashcan and started devouring it. Just as he was about coming out of the trashcan, he saw a decaying bone that had some flesh on it. Its sight was so tempting that he could not resist taking a bite from it. He picked it up and started eating it inside the trashcan. As if someone or something hit him on his head, he felt empty inside and started feeling dizzy.

"What is happening to me?" Ghoulbraham said as he struggled out of the trashcan still holding the bone in his right hand. He held his head with his both hands, staggered and then fell on the floor. A palace guard that was on night patrol saw him as he struggled to get his big feet on the ground. He quickly went inside to call on other guards so they would attack Ghoulbraham. Ghoulbraham could not see them coming as his eyes were now blurred. All he could hear was footsteps approaching him.

"Are you sure that is Ghoul, the creature that has been terrorizing our community and bringing upon us the wrath of the gods?" One of the guards asked the guard that came to call them.

"Yes, if he is not Ghoul, then why does he look like Ghoul?" The guard replied as he brought out his weapon from his sheath.

"Let us stop all this question-and-answer class and kill him before he will regain himself." Another guard said.

Although Ghoulbraham could hear them, his dizziness made him think he was in a trance and what he was hearing was not true. He was still in this when one of the guards gave him a punch on his left cheek and another cut his skin with the sword he was holding. Ghoulbraham could not fight back because fighting back would be him fighting the thin air because he could not see them. He closed his eyes and wished he was back in the stinky forbidden forest. Before the guard with sword would stab him, Ghoulbraham had disappeared from their sights.

"What! he can disappear?" One of the guards exclaimed.

"Do not worry partner, no matter where he disappeared to, we know for sure that he will not last the night and my reasons are because he ate the poisoned trash, he has wounds, and we called him the name he forbids. So my brothers, cheer up and let us keep the good news for our king. He definitely will smile at it tomorrow morning." The guard that was about striking Ghoulbraham told the others.

16

At the stinky forbidden forest Ghoulbraham teleported himself to top of the tree because he was scared that the guards would invade the forest and catch him unaware. He wondered what was wrong with him. He called on his parents to come out and tell him what was happening to him, but they never did. at this point, he knew his death was few seconds away from him for he was all alone. He closed his eyes with tears coming out of his three eyes remembering his parents, Gayu and Zizo who promised to always watched over him.

Soon, Ghoulbraham fell into what seemed to be a trance. In this state of his, he saw the aged woman been taken away by some palace guards at night. They took her to the palace and then presented her to the chief priest and King Katinu. He saw King Katinu questioning the aged woman on his where about, and when she told the king, she did not know where Ghoulbraham was, the chief priest asked King Katinu to order her execution and then feast on her cooked flesh so he would become more powerful to the extent that even Ghoulbraham could not kill him.

He saw when the king killed the old woman, then ate her flesh and then threw the bones into the trash can. When he woke up, he started having the sensation of smoking because he had eaten the bone of the aged woman and she smoked while she was alive. So, he decided to try it. He walked to a tree, cut some dried leaves, and then wrapped it. He looked around to see what he would use to light up the wrapped leaves but he did not find anything. He then decided to go further into the forest to look for stones that he would use to make fire to light up the leaves. He went further into the forest to get a stone and when he got it, he made fire with it and started smoking.

At first, he choked because he has never done it before. But later on, he smoked properly without choking. As he was smoking, the thought of causing havoc between Inoko village and the other village came into his mind.

"But how can I carry out my plans?" He said to himself.

Then the thought of going to the next village to kill the princess and then bring her body to Inoko entered his mind. He smiled and said to himself that the thought that entered his mind was a good one but first had to visit the king's palace at night to check if there were any rotten things there to eat and so after smoking, he slept.

***

At midnight he woke up and went to the king's palace, on getting there, he saw some guards who were sleeping on their duty post. He silently walked pass them and went to the balcony of the palace in search of food. When he got there, he searched gently but saw few rotten foods. He ate it, after eating he became weak because the food was not enough and the food was poisoned. He managed to leave the balcony, on getting to the frontage, he became weaker but he still insisted on leaving the palace. But as he was walking sluggishly out of the palace, his left leg tripped on a stone and almost fell down, this woke the guards up.

On seeing him, the ones that were with spears started throwing their spears at him, while others with sword started running towards him. When he found out that he could not run because he was weak, he disappeared. The guards seeing him that he was weak and then disappeared, assumed that he would die and so they rejoiced and waited eagerly for the following day so they would tell King Katinu.

***

When it was daytime, the guards were the first people to see the king. They knocked at his door and he open and they greeted him. King Katinu told them that he heard voices at night, so one of the guards told him that Ghoulbraham came at night and ate the rotten foods in the waste bin and that as he was leaving, they attacked him and killed him with their swords and spears. The king was not convinced yet that Ghoulbraham was dead not until the other guards confirmed it and told the king that it was true that Ghoulbraham was dead.

The king jumped up for joy.

"This is the best news I have ever received in my entire life." King Katinu said, smiling at the guard that delivered the message to him.

He called on his messenger then instructed him to go and inform everyone in the community that the village would be having a big feast the following day in celebration to the death of the one who had brought great calamities to the village. The messenger greeted and then ran out of the palace to deliver King Katinu's message. After delivering the message to the people, though it was winter, the sun was still scotching them, a thing which had never happened in the history of Inoko for Inoko was among the communities that enjoyed the weather whenever it was winter. the king's messenger decided to have a stop under a sycamore tree to take a rest, not knowing that Ghoulbraham was on the tree watching him.

As the rested, he fell asleep and Ghoulbraham jumped down from the tree with cigarette between his fingers. He put it in his mouth and then lit it. After taking a deep draw from the cigarette, he made a rope from the stem of the sycamore tree on which the messenger was sleeping under. With the leafy rope, he tied the messenger's hands and feet together and then teleported him to the stinky forbidden forest. It was evening and preparations for the following day's celebration was ongoing, yet King Katinu was not himself as he worried about the messenger who was yet to return from the message he was sent by the king.

King Katinu called his guards, he asked them if they had seen his messenger but they all gave him a negative respond. One of palace guards told the king that the messenger might have gone to start his own celebration as the news of Ghoulbraham's death was worth celebrating and not waiting for the following day. The guards said smiling at King Inoko who nodded his head in agreement to what he said.

Ghoulbraham who was now looking much older than his age, puffed out smoke from the cigarette he was smoking while sitting on the lifeless body of the messenger. He took another draw from the cigarette and then took a glance on the body he was sitting on.

"Sorry I did this to you son; you were not good yet your offenses were not like that of your fellow kinsmen. Even though you were the one that led the guards to the aged woman's hut, I say you forgive me for what I did to you. To show you that my punishing you was not intentional, I will not wait for your body to decay so I would have a feel of it. I have better plans for you, plans that every inhabitant of Inoko will benefit from them." Ghoulbraham said tapping the corpse of the messenger who was still under bounds. "Do you care having a draw from my cigarette?" Ghoulbraham asked as he placed the cigarette on the lips of the messenger and then gave a wicked laugh that shook the entire forest.

After laughing for some seconds, he stood up from the body and then placed it on his shoulder. He sniffed in the stinky smell of the forbidden forest, and then started walking out of the forbidden forest.

17

It was night when Ghoulbraham got to Atino still carrying the lifeless body of King Katinu's messenger on his shoulder. Atino was a community that was known for its strength in battle. History had it that Atino never lost any battle to another community, no matter how powerful the community might be.

In Atino, everyone is a warrior. Even the newly born child once he started walking, was trained for battle. To be a king in Atino, one must travel to the land of the unknown where beasts dwelt, kill seven beasts, then bring the heads of the beasts for all to see. It was not an easy task so no one ventured embarking on it, only those that are of blood did because royalty had made them to be without choice.

The lady that was chatting with Zizo and later found dead in Inoko was from Atino. Another thing that the people of Atino was known for was their riches and that was because everyone in the community loved to work. Ghoulbraham walked into the palace of the king of Atino, ignoring all the smells that came out of the trash-cans in Atino. He dropped the lifeless body of King Katinu's messenger in front of the palace in such a way that it made a sound that caught the attention of the guards that were patrolling the palace.

The guards, who were fully armed, rushed out to the front of the palace from where the sound came from. On getting to it, they saw Ghoulbraham smoking with one of his legs on the messenger's corpse. Thinking the corpse was one of them, they charged at Ghoulbraham. It was a fierce fight between them and Ghoulbraham with Ghoulbraham disappearing and appearing.

Although the fight was fierce, it did not take Ghoulbraham two minutes to rip out their hearts from their bodies. Ghoulbraham smiled as he went around the bodies to confirm they were all dead. After the confirmation, he brought out his cigarette from what seemed to be a pocket on his skin. He lit it and after taking a draw from it, he jumped into the trashcan that stood in front of him like it was taking record of what transpired between Ghoulbraham and the guards.

"The meal in this can tastes better than the one in King Katinu's trashcan!" Ghoulbraham said as he continued devouring the trash in the trashcan. When he was fully satisfied, he jumped out of the trashcan and then headed for hut that was separate from the king's palace. He sniffed as he walked towards it with evil smile written all over his face.

The hut was that of the princess of Atino, the only child of the king. The princess was the most beautiful maiden in Atino, as a matter of fact, her beauty earned her the nickname 'THE BRIGHT ONE'. Everyone in Atino especially the males in the community desired to have her as a wife but because she was below the age of getting married, her father did not give her out to anyone. When Ghoulbraham got to the door of the hut, he sniffed again, and then vanished into the room. Seconds later, he came out carrying the lifeless body of the princess on his shoulder with blood dripping from her neck from whence Ghoulbraham killed her.

"When I first thought about this community, I thought it was better than Inoko, I did not know that it is worse than Inoko. Your father and his people kill others for fun, they organize games where they asked their vassals to fight with the freeborn of the land, promising to free them of servitude if they win. But when they win, instead of the getting the freedom that was promised them, they get the freedom of life and a quick passage to the afterlife. The vassal that was bold enough to appreciate your beauty was killed by your father." Ghoulbraham said looking at the body on his shoulder. "Your body will serve as a game for your father and Katinu." Ghoulbraham said with an appearance that hid his feelings.

He took a last glance on the lifeless bodies in front of the palace and then disappeared with the lifeless body of the king's daughter.

***

It was a beautiful morning in Inoko and all the gifts of nature were at their bests... the birds were singing joyfully; the trees were dancing seriously even though there was no song that was playing. The air was fresh and cool, one that Inoko never experienced for a very long time.

"You see what I told you last night my king?" The guard that spoke to King Katinu the previous night told King Katinu as both of them went around the palace to inspect the preparations that were on for the feast of Ghoulbraham.

"I do not know what is happening to me, I feel kind of empty inside of me." King Katinu told the guard who advised he needed to have some rest before the celebration would start as he was still suffering from the death of the chief priest.

King Katinu smiled at the guard, he thanked him for his advice, then ordered him to supervise the preparations. As King Katinu walked to the front of his palace wondering why he was feeling empty and why his messenger was yet to return to the palace, a guard whom he had sent to go and search for his messenger, returned with his hands on his head.

"Why are your hands on your head? Did something happen to my messenger?" King Katinu asked the guard with an expression that showed he was worried.

"My Lord, I combed the entire community but did not see your messenger, but saw the corpse of the princess of Atino in our community." The guard told King Katinu still placing his hands on his head.

Upon hearing this, king Katinu ordered the guard to take some other guards with him to where he saw the lifeless body of the princess.

"When you get there, bury her as fast as you can. And after that, gather all the strong men of this community and report back to the palace." King Katinu told the guard.

The guard bowed, then ran out to carry out the king's order.

"Her father is not going to forgive us this time around!" King Katinu said as he turned and headed for his chamber.

Meanwhile, there was pandemonium in Atino with everyone calling for war against Inoko after discovering the body of King Katinu's messenger at the palace of their king, the bodies of some of the palace guards, and blood stains on the leafy bed of the princess. The king's eyes were so red that one would think they produce blood and not tears.

"They did it the first time and because I did nothing, they did this." The king said pointing at the bloodstain on the bed of his daughter.

He moved to his armory, pulled out a weapon and turning at the guards that were beside him, he declared war against Inoko kingdom and everyone jumped in jubilation.

***

Less than thirty minutes, the bravest men in Inoko had gathered at King Katinu's palace. He told them what one of the guards discovered. His narration equally sent fear into the hearts of the people. He tasked them to brace themselves and prepare for battle because either they chose to fight or not, the warriors of Atino were going to invade the community and then made it desolate.

"My gallant warriors, fight for yourself and for your family because It is better you fight and let the gods of the land make you vic-
torious than for you to allow your children and family taken away
into captivity and you know what the king of Atino does to his vassals." King Katinu told the warriors with hard face.

"My lord, do you want us to attack the Atino now or guard our
community so the warriors of Atino will not be able to invade our
community?" One of the warriors said, making a fist.

King Katinu ordered them to attack Atino now before they
would plan and then attack Inoko. The guards and the warriors
chanted war songs as they marched out of the palace. A day that was
supposed to be filled with merriments in Inoko, turned out to be the
day when everyone living in the community was filled with fright.

Ghoulbraham smiled as he took a bite of the decaying meal he
had taken from one of the trashcans he jumped into and devoured
in Inoko after returning from Atino.

18

It was a weather with mixed appearance as although the sun was shining and the wind was blowing cool. The atmosphere was cloudy, making it look as if the god of the atmosphere was aware that there was going to be loss of lives that day as warriors from both Atino and Inoko went up to the border that separated them to battle with each other. Meanwhile, Ghoulbraham had teleported himself to the border where he hid himself in the thick garbage fence that was there, eating and watching the warriors as they battled with each other.

Ghoulbraham did not smoke while he ate in the garbage fence because he did not want the smoke to draw the attention of any of the warriors to him. He did not even make a sound as he enjoyed his meal. The garbage fence was actually gathered there by King Katinu while he wanted to prevent Atino from gaining entrance into his community, and his inhabitants from moving over to Atino.

He halted the building of the thick garbage fence not because the people that were building it complained about the awful smell that was oozing out from it, but because Inoko lived in peace with Atino. And after the death of the maiden Zizo was talking to at one of the evenings and the king of Atino forgave them, he thought nothing would make them battle with each other. If not for the halting of the garbage fence, nothing would have made the Atinos think of ever fighting with them, or if they ever thought of that, before they would have gained entrance into Inoko, all the inhabitants of Inoko would have successfully relocated to wherever they ever wanted to go. As a matter of fact, it was because of this that the Inokos started keeping trash in their homes in trashcans.

The battle was so fierce as the warriors of Inoko fought like never before. They fought with all their might believing their gods would favor them, but, alas, nothing of such happened. As a matter of fact, their fighting skill only made room for the anger that was in the hearts of the Atino's warriors burn harder. They fought back using all the weapons at their disposals and knowing that if they did not get victory, they would be killed by their king because their king has ordered them not to return to the community without killing all the warriors of Inoko.

It was a battle that started in the morning under the cloudy weather until in the noon when it started raining snow. Like the rain of snow was a mark to end the battle between both warriors, the warriors of Atino, lay around the border dead with only a few of the Atino's warriors dead.

Ghoulbraham was still enjoying himself inside the thick fence when he heard a loud sound of victory from the battlefield. He peeped through one of the holes in the wall of the thick garbage fence and saw that the sound of victory actually came from the warriors of Atino.

"Hail yourselves!" The commander of the Atino warriors told his fellow warriors and they all did. "We have made our king proud and have given meaning to the community we came from. Now the people of Inoko are vulnerable as all their men of might are no more. This is the best time to attack it, I mean to attack and kill everyone in it as it is our culture." The commander further spoke raising up his weapon.

One of the warriors suggested they did not attack the Inokos as their great king did not give them the order to, he only ordered them to attack and kill all the warriors of Inoko and that they had done. He made them remember that going against the king's order or doing what he did not order they do was usually punishable by death. At this, all the warriors returned to Atino, chatting war songs.

The warriors of Atino returned to their fully armed king who was already waiting for them at the community square with another sect of warriors should they not be able to defeat the warriors of Inoko.

With a warlord tone of voice, he asked the warriors what the outcome of the battle was. And when he was told, he turned his back and went home, instructing everyone that was around him to retire to their abodes as they would be paying Inoko a visit the following day returning with the head of King Katinu. None dared suggesting they invaded Inoko that same day because they were scared of asking him and they were exhausted after the battle with the Inokos.

***

There is a popular saying, which says that evil news usually spread like wide fires. None went with the warriors of Inoko to the border to battle with the warriors of Atino, but barely had the warriors of Atino returned to their community when king Katinu received the heartbreaking news. The news was indeed heartbreaking as it made King Katinu develop heartache. He sat on his royal leafy chair contemplating on what to do because he knew that his community was now vulnerable and would be attacked by the king of Atino.

Even in his heartache, everyone in the community left their homes for his palace as they all wanted to die together in the view of everyone especially their king. They were still in the presence of

King Katinu when Ghoulbraham walked into the palace, carrying a decaying food in his left hand and cigarette in the fingers of his left hand. Everyone including King Katinu was scared because the last time they saw him, he was not as big as he now looked, some had not seen him and all of them thought he was long dead.

As they wondered, Ghoulbrahaam put his cigarette in his mouth, lit it as he moved closer to King Katinu and his people making them to be more afraid.

"I know what happened and what is about happening to this community before the end of tomorrow if nothing is done about it now." Ghoulbraham finally spoke after puffing out smoke from his mouth.

"I do not understand what you are trying to say Ghoul." King Katinu spoke.

"Hahaha! You called me Ghoul thinking it will bring an end to my existence, and I was trying to help you and your community. Why?" Ghoulbraham spoke, taking a bite from the meat in his hand.

"It is better we die in the hands of the Atinos than for we to die in the hands of a cruel beast like you." An age man that was in the gathering of the people at King Katinu's palace, spoke.

"I came here to help my community out from the doom that hovers around it, and I thought I would meet some good people that have hope for the future, not knowing that the ones with good hearts and hope for the future died today." Ghoulbraham said taking a smoke and then turned to take his leave when King Katinu called him.

"What do you have in mind son?" king Katinu asked standing up from his seat.

"I want you to send me to send me to Atino so I will bring upon them what they have planned bringing on us." Ghoulbraham replied King Katinu with his face facing the entrance of the compound that housed the palace.

"I do not think you will succeed but if you do, you will rule over Inoko since my days on earth are almost out." King Katinu said trying to lay his right hand on Ghoulbraham but was taken aback by the smell of the meat he was eating.

"Are you sure about what you just said my king?" Ghoulbraham asked throwing away cigarette.

"The past kings of Inoko never went back on their words; I am not going to be the one that would start it. Go, and if you ever succeed, you will know if I lied on my promises." King Katinu said as he returned back to his seat.

Ghoulbraham having a long distance before he would get to Atino community, walked out of the palace not wanting the people to know that he could disappear. And as soon as he was out of sight, he disappeared.

The people that were with King Katinu asked him if he was sure about the promise he made to Ghoulbraham.

"I made those promises to him because I am very sure he is not going to return alive." King Katinu answered with a smile that was later followed with a sad look for he remembered that their life span on earth would last just for a day.

It was evening but the sun was yet to set in Atino. The king of Atino and his warlords were at the palace planning how to invade Inoko in the early hours of the following day. The king gave a standing order not to take any inhabitants of Inoko as vassals, no matter their gender or age. He instructed them to kill everyone including the newly born because if they were not killed, they would someday grow and want to avenge the death of their loved ones.

Because of their plans and when they would be carried out, the king ordered everyone not to return home but to pass the night in his palace. He was still instructing his warriors when Ghoulbraham appeared at the rear of the palace. He looked around to see if anyone was around. When he was sure no one was around, he sneaked

into the trashcan to have continue from where he stopped the previous night. After having his feel, he disappeared and then appeared
in the kitchen where the meals that were to be served to the king
and his warriors were on fire. Ghoulbraham pulled out a tube-like
substance from his skin, which he emptied into the meal. He gave a
wicked laugh and then disappeared.

When they had finished the meeting, the king of Atino ordered
his meal and that of his warriors be served in large quantity as they
would not have the time for meal the following day. His order was
carried out. His warriors ate in silence as they could see visible tears
coking down the cheeks of their king. They wished he never lost his
daughter but could not console him because of his present condition.

It was midnight and the stars were shining bright in the sky.
The palace was so quiet that one could hear the croaking of frogs.
Ghoulbraham walked into the palace like someone who had just
won a jackpot. He walked into the rooms that were in the palace
ripping out the hearts of the people inside the rooms.

Though some of the people saw Ghoulbraham entering into
rooms before he ripped out their hearts, they lay helpless on their
beds as the potency of the substance that Ghoulbraham put into
their meals was already working inside them. It was indeed really an
easy task for Ghoulbraham as he would rip out some hearts, went
out to have some meals in the trashcans and then returned to continue with his execution.

After killing everyone that was in the palace, including the king,
Ghoulbraham went into the community to kill everyone that was of
age for battle, turning Atino into a community for the toddlers, he
did not even spare the aged ones and the women of the community.
When he was done with his execution, he stood at the center of the
community, gave a sigh of relief, brought out his cigarette and then
had a long smoke before walking out of the center of the commu-

nity. One could easily hear the wailing of the toddlers of the community.

Although Ghoulbraham was very weak, he still had some strength with which he carried a trashcan and then disappeared out of the community into the stinky forbidden forest. That night was one of the best nights for Ghoulbraham as he ate and drank the liquor, the ones took from Atino to his satisfaction.

***

It was morning, King Katinu and the people that were with him at his palace woke up to see that they were still alive, not dead as they had presumed. They jumped up in jubilation thanking the gods for sparing their lives. Some of them even went as far as bowing to King Katinu making look as if he was the one that made them see the day. King Katinu could be everything bad, but one thing he was not was taking another man's glory.

He asked his people not to thank him for he was not the one that made them to see that day but the gods. He also told them not to be over joyous as the day was still young and anything could still happen to them.

"We can only be happy when we see the end of today, for I am very sure the Atinos will strike before the sun would set on us. Let us eat all we can eat now so that we will not be hungry in the afterlife." King Katinu said wearing a long face.

He was about calling on the palace maid to prepare their breakfast when Ghoulbraham walked into the palace in a manner of a warlord that had just won battle.

"What is going on here? Why are you people not celebrating king Katinu?" Ghoulbraham asked as he continued walking towards the king.

"Celebrating you say? Why will we celebrate and to what are we celebrating?" King Katinu asked Ghoulbraham who replied his question with a smile that revealed his big set of teeth.

"You have every reason to celebrate because the people who planned to put an end to your community are no more." Ghoulbraham said in a proud manner.

"What did you just say Ghoul?" King Katinu asked pushing his face forward.

Ghoulbraham told him that the Atinos were no more and that it was time for him to give meaning to the promises he made to him the previous day, but organize a celebration that would last the day for they would be having many years to live on earth. Not believing what Ghoulbraham told them about the Atinos, King Katinu asked some of the young ones to go to Atino and confirm what Ghoulbraham had said and like a swift wind, four young stars stood up and ran out of the palace.

Ghoulbraham did not bother about them or about the king, he walked to one end of the palace and then took a sit on the leafy chair that was there waiting for the young stars to return. He brought out his cigarette and then had a smoke with the eyes of everyone fixed on him. After getting done with the cigarette in his fingers, he walked to the trashcan that was at the other side of the palace. He peered into it and saw that nothing was in it.

He walked up to another trashcan and discovered it was same with the first one.

"Why are these trashcans empty King Katinu?" Ghoulbraham asked with a serious face.

"We have neither prepared nor fed for the past two days now. But we planned doing that today so we will not be hungry in the afterlife." King Katinu replied him, wearing a long face as well.

Ghoulbraham looked at him from his head down to his toes. He warned King Katinu to always make sure there were trash in the trashcans when he becomes his palace messenger. At this, King Katinu and the people with him burst into laugh.

"I will advise you wait for the crown before you start thinking of how it would look on you." One of the people spoke up.

Ghoulbraham did not mind what they were saying; he just went back to his sitting position, sat with his legs crossed. Few hours later, the young stars that went to Atino returned with bloodstains on their bodies, and everyone including King Katinu ran up to them to question them on their findings.

The young stars looked at each other and then jumped up in excitement while Ghoulbraham watched them from his sitting position. They told them that the king, his warriors, and everyone in Atino were dead, that the only people that they found alive in Atino were their toddlers who could do nothing other than to cry.

"Yes, my king, and we killed every one of them with the swords of the warriors because we did not want a situation where they would grow avenge the death of..." One of the young stars was still talking when Ghoulbraham like a swift wind, ripped out his heart and that of the other young stars.

"I spared their lives because they were vulnerable, yet you all went there and killed them because they were vulnerable." Ghoulbraham said squeezing the heart that was in his right hand as he moved around the dead bodies of the young stars on the ground.

Turning to King Katinu, he ordered him to hand over his crown and throne to him else he would face same fate as the young stars.

"Off course I will do just as you have said." King Katinu said with smile on his face.

Ghoulbraham smiled back at him, he told him that he would make Katinu his palace messenger and then make sure everyone in the community enjoyed being alive as he would protect them from all impending doom. He also promised bringing upon the community the blessings of the gods by making their crops grow well and then make the sun cool. The people liked everything he said he would do except the one where he said he would make the king his palace messenger.

They could not ask Ghoulbraham his reasons for they were scared of what he would do to them.

"Why you wonder how your new king would bring to life all." he said, "I say we have a celebration to our freedom from the evil Atino."

The people jumped up in excitement and this made Ghoulbraham smile. And it was so.

It was not up to a week Ghoulbraham became the king of Inoko the palace was already filled with awful smell of trash as he had turned his palace into a dumpsite for trash, threatening anyone that failed to bring his or her trash to his palace with death. He made it compulsory for everyone to visit his palace and have some deep inhaling of the trash knowing they could not bear inhaling it for too long a time and still have appetite for food at home.

Although Ghoulbraham was enjoying his reign as king as he could eat whatever kind of trash he desired, the people suffered a lot from him. Each time they gathered to plan how they would over throne Ghoulbraham, he would summon the culprits and even after confessing to the crime, Ghoulbraham still had them executed before the eyes of everyone. His executioner was also King Katinu who could not question the order given to him by Ghoulbraham because he had once seen him appear from nowhere wearing a sad look.

What he did not know was that Ghoulbraham was summoned by other gods who warned him to stop doing what he was doing after killing some people who were innocent of the crime Ghoulbraham accused them of because he saw them as threat to his reign. And when he refused to desist from what they warned him to, the eldest amongst the gods, cursed him by telling him that his stay has been shortened and that his secret name would be made known to a lesser being. This made him sad, as he wanted to stay until the end of everyone in the community.

Everything seemed to have been forgotten by Ghoulbraham until a day when he wanted to kill an aged man who could not come to the palace to have his own share of the inhaling of the awful smell of the palace. the aged man had been ill for some days after slipping on his way from the palace.

"My king, I could not come to the palace yesterday because I was down in health. Please forgive me." The man begged Ghoulbraham who did not pay listening ears to his plea but went ahead to order the execution of the aged man.

"GHOULBRAHAM, son of ZIZO, son of BRAHAM, please forgive me." The aged man spoke as King Katinu raised up his sword to strike him.

There was thunder blast in the palace that severed Ghoulbraham's body into different particles. A heavy whirlwind from nowhere appeared in the palace spinning Ghoulbraham's severed body in it before the eyes of everyone, and in no time, disappeared with Ghoulbraham. The people of Inoko jumped in jubilation because they knew the meaning of the event the event that took place.

Ghoulbraham appeared at the front of a shop in Colorado with so much anger of not accomplishing his mission, as he was walking thinking of how to pour out his anger on the people of Colorado, he stumbled into Chicho another female creature. They both fell to the ground and when they got up, Ghoulbraham was astonished at the sight of Chicho.

He quickly stood up and gave her a lifting hand and as she stood up, he helped her dust off her body and Chicho apologized for hitting him mistakenly but he cut her short by saying he is to be sorry for not watching where he was actually going to. Chicho smiled and told him it was okay.

Ghoulbraham introduced himself to her and asked them to be friends, Chicho accepted and introduced herself too then she asked him where he was going to? He said nowhere in particular. He asked her where she was going to too? And she replied that she was a thrift collector and owned a thrift shop. She said she was actually going to start savings for that day when they stumbled into themselves.

Ghoulbraham asked if he could join her and assist in case she needed any assistance. Chicho smiled and replied saying he was right as she will be needing someone to assist and equally keep her company. They both walked to the shop. Chicho opened up and Ghoulbraham helped her in arranging the goods. Apart from being a thrift collector, Chicho sold flowers in her shop but that day, there was no sale. Chicho was already feeling bad about it when Ghoulbraham noticed. He asked her to close her eyes and make a wish and she wished she had lots of sales. Ghoulbraham granted her wish and under few minutes, they were lots of people coming to get flowers.

She sold and sold that she could no longer handle it and she begged Ghoulbraham to assist which he did smiling. It got to an extent she turned the shop instruction to close. Many others came and she said they had closed for the day. She turned to Ghoulbraham and asked him how he did it. He acted like he did not understand but Chicho asked him not to lie to her and reminded him of how he asked her to make a wish which came to pass even beyond her imagination. He then told her who he really was but asked her not to reveal to anyone.

He said he naturally does evil but felt something soft immediately he saw her. He equally said he had anger issues. After telling her, he stood up and tried leaving but Chicho asked him to stop and he stood. She walked up to him, held his hands and told that there was still something good in him, she kissed Ghoulbraham softly and stars gathered in the sky. They both went to Chicho's house. They started living together, doing things together and went to the shop together. Every night while Chicho was asleep, Ghoulbraham would disappear into the city, scouting for trashcans that he would feed on, and have some nice smoke for although he ate normal meal with Chicho who was everything about Ghoulbraham except the eating of trash and rotten food, the ability to disappear and the smoking of cigarette, he was never satisfied.

Chicho started making wild sales and lots of people started saving their money with her. It was so much that she became the talk of Colorado, then some started envying her and thought of what to do to get at her. They decided to burn down her shop to make her feel bad. That faithful evening after Chicho and Ghoulbraham had closed for the day, they left the shop for their home and then came Fako and her team, blue creatures.

Fako used to be the one making all the sales with the aid of her team, a team that did evil to everyone they saw as threat to their success story. They were usually nice looking during the day, exhibiting all the characters of an angel so their evil deeds would not be noticed by anyone, but at night, they would transform their kindness into hatred.

So, they first stood outside the shop so that passersby who did not know them would think they were either waiting for someone, or the owner of the shop. While they stood, Fako whispered into the ears of two of the girls in her team and when she was done, the two girls hurried out of the scene. Minutes later, they returned with two gallons that had liquid inside of them. They all laughed at each other, then asked Fako when they would execute their plans. Fako told them to wait for the day to become darker before they would execute their plans.

Meanwhile, Chicho slept and snored, Ghoulbraham could not. He was restless in the bed he was laying. He wondered what the problem was but was never successful on his wondering.

"I am not hungry and do not feel like taking something into my stomach or could it be that it is because I have not smoked today, I am restless?" Ghoulbraham soliloquized in a low tone so he will not wake up Chicho.

As he soliloquized, he remembered he had forgotten his cigarette in a drawer at the shop while he was rushing to close the shop and meet Chicho outside.

"Oh!" He exclaimed, then turned to look at Chicho who was enjoying her sleep due to the heavy workloads at the shop that day.

After satisfying himself that she was still sleeping and would not wake up until after many hours, he disappeared from the room, leaving Chicho alone in the room. He appeared in front of a house that was in the same street with Chicho's shop. He saw Fako and her team standing in front of the shop. He wondered what they were doing there and as he attempted to walk up to them, he smelt the awful smell that was coming out of the trashcan that was in the house. The smell reminded him of the nicest meal he ever ate and that was the one ate in Atino.

He moved closer to the trashcan as the awful smell was so inviting. Ignoring Fako and her girls, he jumped into the trashcan and feasted on the trash that was in the trashcan. When he was full, he came out of the trashcan but did not see Fako and her team of girls in front of the shop, but the two gallons that had liquid in them and what seemed to be a matchbox on one of the gallons.

What he saw made him not to wonder anymore the plans of Fako as the entrance door of her shop was wide opened and he could hear their voices inside.

"To my markers and the ones who are older than I am, I hope you forgive me what I am about doing to these little humans." Ghoulbraham said raising his hands up and when he was done with what seemed to be a prayer request to the higher ones, he gave a wicked smile, then strolled to the shop.

At the shop, Fako and her team were busy ransacking everywhere in the shop.

"Have you seen any money yet?" Fako asked one of her girls who was busy searching the drawers.

She gave Fako a negative answer and the other girls that were not asked the question also gave negative answers.

"I think she does not keep her clients' money here. However, if we do not see any money in the next two minutes, we shall execute the second plan, which is to burn down the shop. Hope you all understood?" Fako asked the girls and before they would answer 'yes,' Ghoulbraham answered he 'no' as he stood in front of the entrance door.

"Who said no?" Fako asked raising up her head.

And when she saw Ghoulbraham, there was a surprise look on her face and on the faces of the other girls who first saw Ghoulbraham.

"What is there that you want to understand ugly thing?" Fako blasted Ghoulbraham who stood still at the entrance with his eyes fixed on them.

"I do not want to understand what you little beings are trying to do to this shop, what I understand is that if you little beings do not leave this shop this minute, you may not be lucky to get another chance." He replied to Fako. "Can you please give me my cigarette that I left in that drawer?" Ghoulbraham asked the girl that was standing behind the drawer.

She gave him a positive answer.

Making an attempt to open the drawer that was no longer there but, on the floor, because she had thrown it away while she was searching for money, she pulled a knife and then threw it at Ghoulbraham who dodged it and with a speed of light.

He ripped out her heart as he appeared in front of her, not giving Fako and the other girls the ability to see that he could vanish. Upon seeing what Ghoulbraham had done to one of them, they all charged at Ghoulbraham like wounded lions.

They fought like the warriors of Atino but because of their numbers, could not defeat Ghoulbraham who ripped out their hearts as well, leaving Fako who was by now exhausted as a result of the fight he had with Ghoulbraham.

She begged Ghoulbraham for mercy but her plea fell on deaf ears as Ghoulbraham did not only rip out her heart, he started by removing other valuable organs making sure that she suffered in pains before finally ripping out her heart.

"Now this place is all messed up and I need to return to Chicho before she would notice I am not around and then become worried. I cannot afford her or anyone see this mess else her shop which she cherished most will be closed by the government of this city." Ghoulbraham said with a worrisome look.

As he looked around trying to figure out what decision to make, the shop started transforming into the way it was before it was invaded by Fako and her team. This got Ghoulbraham confused because he was not the one that was behind the transformation that was going on for although he was blessed with some powers, the power of transforming things back to what they were was not part of it. As he watched in amazement, a familiar voice spoke from the soft breeze that was blowing in the shop, thanking him for saving the shop. And as he wondered more, Chicho appeared from the breeze wearing a smile Ghoulbraham had never seen in his entire life.

"You think you are the only one with powers?" She asked Ghoulbraham who had forgotten that his mouth was wide opened.

She walked closer to Ghoulbraham then planted her lips on Ghoulbraham's lips that lasted for some minutes while her shop was still transforming. **THE END**